"In *Becoming Brave*, Dr. McNeil exercises uncommon courage. Part confession, part biblical reflection, part call to storm the gates, *Becoming Brave* declares that the Christian call to do justice cannot and shall no longer be guided, shaped, and defanged by sensibilities more loyal to white people's comfort than to God. McNeil has led two generations of evangelical Christians into the value and practice of racial reconciliation. With *Becoming Brave* she returns and calls her followers to gird their courage and engage like never before, for the sake of the gospel. This book is a must-read."

—**Lisa Sharon Harper**, founder and president, Freedom Road

"Brenda Salter McNeil has been a giant in the work of racial reconciliation among evangelicals. Like Tom Skinner and Bill Pannell in previous generations, she defines for this generation of evangelical scholars and pastors what real racial reconciliation means on the ground. There is simply no one who has worked with more thoughtfulness, theological precision, and faithfulness at this vital work than Brenda Salter McNeil. There is no one who understands more clearly what is necessary to move white evangelicals forward beyond their racial captivity than McNeil, and there is no more important book that must find its way into the hands of students, pastors, Christian activists, and all those who understand the urgency of this moment than *Becoming Brave*."

—**Willie James Jennings**, professor, Yale Divinity School; author of *After Whiteness: An Education in Belonging*

"This is a beautiful and courageous book about journeys. Brenda Salter McNeil takes us on hers, even as she invites us to newly understand Queen Esther's and—ultimately—our own. Real prophets lovingly criticize and truthfully energize. McNeil does both with clarity and with the kind of rare vulnerability that—when offered by a justice leader in it for the long haul and deeply responding to God's call—enables the rest of us to get quiet and ask again what it is that God requires of us.

This book will move your heart and compel your feet to move as well, with others, in response to God's call to do justice."

—Jennifer Harvey, author of *Raising White Kids: Bringing Up Children in a Racially Unjust America*

"During a time requiring moral clarity and moral courage, Dr. Brenda Salter McNeil calls any and all with ears to hear to be brave. Through a combination of personal reflection, cultural awareness, and biblical exegesis of the book of Esther, she provides a roadmap for leaders to become and to be brave."

—Bishop Claude Alexander, senior pastor, The Park Church, Charlotte, North Carolina

"Dr. Brenda Salter McNeil explicates that to speak about the centrality of justice in the story of God and in the gospel of Jesus Christ is to speak about the wet part of the ocean. A Christlike church cannot depart from Christlike justice. She urges the church to grow in the paradigm of racial justice and reconciliation into what the Spirit is calling the church to be now. For such a time as this: a just church that repairs broken systems. With over thirty years of ministry experience as a reconciler, she walks us through her own growth and development of a racial reconciliation paradigm with honesty, candor, challenge, and kingdom urgency using the courageous story of Esther. This book is light in our darkness and an urgent, prophetic wake-up call to a church that has lost its reconciling credibility."

—Inés Velásquez-McBryde, pastor, speaker, and reconciler; chaplain, Fuller Theological Seminary

"There is not a more credible, seasoned, and dynamic voice in the country that could speak to us about leadership and reconciliation than Rev. Dr. Brenda Salter McNeil. She has guided countless organizations and individuals through these choppy waters, and there are literally thousands of people who could bear testimony to the way she has changed their lives—including me. That is why I cannot recommend *Becoming Brave* strongly enough. In this book you will be equipped and moved to become someone different and better than what you've ever been before."

—Daniel Hill, pastor; author of *White Awake*

"Rev. Brenda illuminates a justice path for those seeking to be brave or simply responding to the times. With truth-telling, vulnerability, and profound scriptural insights, Rev. Brenda's work reflects the complex struggles that come from a long engagement in reconciliation work. In *Becoming Brave*, Rev. Brenda, one of the American church's great leaders of racial reconciliation, delves into the unexpected disruptions she has encountered during her journey toward deep reconciliation. She models and illuminates a path for others. A fantastic resource for advocating for and embodying justice."

—Nikki Toyama-Szeto, executive director, Evangelicals for Social Action at the Sider Center of Eastern University

"Brenda's reflections in *Becoming Brave* could stand in for countless numbers of people in the community of color. For many, the first years of faith disarmed the gospel of its resistance to injustice—the restoration of God's shalom—replacing it with the placating call to piety, to 'Just follow Jesus!' We celebrated soul salvation, our ticket home to a triumphant eternity, with the implicit expectation that earthly matters were important only inasmuch as they ensured we could 'occupy until Jesus returns.' This truncated experience of salvation meant that continuing injustice went unaddressed by many gospel-embracing believers. Clearly, a disarmed gospel is no gospel at all. If we are honest, most people of color can insert their names, stories, and journeys in the place of Brenda's. The gospel we initially responded to was about soul salvation and piety. Her stories, rooted in women of action in Scripture, inspire us to deepen our faith and take the whole gospel to the whole of creation. Paul admonishes us that 'the whole of creation awaits the revelation of the children of God.' Perhaps this is less about us being revealed than it is about us experiencing the gospel more fully. In *Becoming Brave*, Brenda challenges us to be woke!"

—Terry LeBlanc, director, NAIITS: An Indigenous
Learning Community

"I want to be a leader for racial reconciliation. Dr. McNeil's book is an essential tool for my leadership education. It is not a book for the faint of heart. Dr. McNeil anchors her wisdom in the book of Esther. And while I was inspired by the wisdom of the book, it's going to challenge you. It pulls no punches. And for these reasons, it is an essential read."

—Shirley Hoogstra, president, Council for Christian
Colleges and Universities

"For years, Dr. McNeil has been a pioneer in awakening churches to the biblical call to racial reconciliation. She is now taking a bold and courageous step forward into new territory. My prayer is that all who have received and appreciated her ministry will follow her into the wilderness—in a parallel journey to that of Moses and Miriam leaving Egypt. In this brilliant and powerful book, Dr. McNeil makes a case for recognizing this kairos moment when traditional reconciliation models don't go far enough to liberate us from fear and captivity. This book is a clarion call that cuts through the fog of our partisan arguments and blazes a path to abundant life for all. All of those who are suffering unjustly at this time need you to read this book and respond. This book will equip you to hear your equivalent to the call of Queen Esther—that you are who you are in order to speak out in your place for such a time as this."

—Alexia Salvatierra, Centro Latino professor, School
of Intercultural Studies, Fuller Theological Seminary

BECOMING
BRAVE

OTHER BOOKS BY BRENDA SALTER MCNEIL

*The Heart of Racial Justice: How Soul Change
Leads to Social Change* (with Rick Richardson)

*A Credible Witness: Reflections on
Power, Evangelism and Race*

*Roadmap to Reconciliation: Moving Communities
into Unity, Wholeness and Justice*

BECOMING
BRAVE

FINDING
THE COURAGE
TO PURSUE
RACIAL JUSTICE
NOW

BRENDA SALTER McNEIL

Brazos Press
a division of Baker Publishing Group
Grand Rapids, Michigan

Published by Brazos Press
a division of Baker Publishing Group
PO Box 6287, Grand Rapids, MI 49516-6287
www.brazospress.com

Printed in the United States of America

Library of Congress Cataloging-in-Publication Data
Names: McNeil, Brenda Salter, 1955– author.
Title: Becoming brave : finding the courage to pursue racial justice now / Brenda Salter McNeil.
Description: Grand Rapids, Michigan : Brazos Press, a division of Baker Publishing Group, 2020.
Identifiers: LCCN 2019052643 | ISBN 9781587434471
Subjects: LCSH: Christianity and justice. | Race relations—Religious aspects—Christianity. | Reconciliation—Religious aspects—Christianity. | Church and minorities.
Classification: LCC BR115.J8 M42 2020 | DDC 261.8—dc23
LC record available at https://lccn.loc.gov/2019052643

Unless otherwise indicated, Scripture quotations are from the Contemporary English Version © 1991, 1992, 1995 by American Bible Society. Used by permission.

Scripture quotations labeled CEB are from the Common English Bible. © Copyright 2011 by the Common English Bible. All rights reserved. Used by permission.

Scripture quotations labeled ISV are from the International Standard Version. Copyright © 1995–2014 by ISV Foundation. All rights reserved internationally. Used by permission of Davidson Press, LLC.

Scripture quotations labeled KJV are from the King James Version of the Bible.

Scripture quotations labeled NIV are from THE HOLY BIBLE, NEW INTERNATIONAL VERSION®, NIV® Copyright © 1973, 1978, 1984, 2011 by Biblica, Inc.® Used by permission. All rights reserved worldwide.

The author is represented by Alive Literary Agency, www.aliveliterary.com.

20 21 22 23 24 25 26   7 6 5 4 3 2 1

green press INITIATIVE

In memory of my spiritual mother, mentor, and friend,
Mrs. Percia A. Hutcherson,
a civil rights and disabilities advocate
and one of the bravest women I've ever known.

It takes courage to grow up and
become who you really are.

E. E. Cummings

CONTENTS

FOREWORD

Austin Channing Brown

WHEN PEOPLE ASK how I met Rev. Dr. Brenda Salter McNeil, I always respond, "Divine intervention." It was a series of fortunate events that landed me in her office, then called Overflow Ministries, interviewing to be her administrative assistant. I was a first-year college student still trying to find my way in the world. As I sat across from her, mesmerized by her gentle but joyful energy, I knew immediately I would take the job. But here is the truth: I had no idea who she was. I didn't know she could preach the roof off a building, speak truth to power, or stir the hearts of anyone feeling lost, dismissed, or unimportant. I didn't know of her deep commitment to young people or her passion for racial reconciliation. By the time I figured out that this woman was changing lives, I was already in love with her.

I could go on for days about the ways that Dr. Brenda has mentored me, taught me, loved me. She mentored me through the sermon-writing process and taught me to leave a tip in hotel rooms. She took me to my first meeting with an editor, years before I was offered a book deal. She has mentored me through some of my hardest moments of navigating white churches and workplaces. For fifteen years she has been fully present in my life. But what is most important for you to know is that the book you are holding is the bravest book Dr. Brenda has ever written. She is brave because she believes in you. You see, when you're the expert in the room, it's really easy to share what you know. What is far more difficult, far more brave, is to share your journey. How did you arrive at your understanding? What did you get wrong before? How was your silence complicity? How have you changed?

In the following pages, Dr. Brenda doesn't bop you over the head, chiding you for not knowing more about justice. Instead, she invites you to be brave with her—to change your mind, to grow, to venture into uncharted territory, because you love oppressed people, marginalized people, God's people. Using the framework of the story of Hadassah (later given the name Esther), Dr. Brenda shares her own story. Where she got it right and where she got it wrong. She offers you her growing pains in hopes that you too will choose growth over stagnation.

It has been my joy to watch Dr. Brenda close-up. I have seen her command a stage and wash dishes. I have watched her pour into the lives of strangers and wipe away her kids' tears. I have been witness to her questions and her answers. Here is what I know for sure: Dr. Brenda longs for justice in the world, and she is not content to silently hope it will one day appear. She is determined to be brave, to speak, to write, to challenge even herself if it means leaning into the pursuit of justice.

If you are reading this, my guess is you have changed a lot in the last few years too. Your heart has softened while your curiosity has grown. You have been reading and studying and changing your mind. You have allowed yourself to feel the pain caused by injustice. And the only question that remains is, *What do I do now?*

Here is Dr. Brenda's answer: It's time to be brave.

PREFACE

"DR. BRENDA, when are you gonna talk about justice?"

It was the last day of a multiday workshop on racial reconciliation. I prayed, I preached, and I gave a call to action. I taught the Bible and told the whole truth about how Jesus's work on the cross not only served as a vertical reconnection to God but also demonstrated the horizontal connection we have to one another. I told the workshop participants how to have more inclusive worship services and extolled the importance of being engaged with and learning from people who look different, speak a different language, or come from a different place than they do.

I had just finished doing all of this when a young African American seminary student asked me this question: "Dr. Brenda, when are you gonna talk about justice?" I thought to myself, *Didn't I just spend several days talking about justice? Didn't I talk about racial justice all the time?* I had been doing this work for over thirty years. I didn't know what he was talking about, but it was clear that he was visibly frustrated with me, and I wasn't sure why. I didn't understand what else he wanted from me. What else could I possibly do?

I mumbled some sort of half-answer to conclude the session but was determined to find the student to ask just what he meant. As we talked afterward, he explained that although he thought the seminar was helpful, he didn't believe I had gone far enough in specifically addressing issues of systemic and structural injustice that affect people of color, the poor, and the marginalized in our society. I had difficulty responding to his question because, frankly, I thought that I already had. In my mind, my entire life's work had been talking about justice. If I hadn't been talking about justice, then what had I been talking about exactly?

I thanked him for his honesty and courage in asking the question. Although I wasn't sure if I agreed with him, I could not get his pointed inquiry out of my mind. Long after I returned home and spoke at other workshops, preached at churches across the country, and taught my classes, I could not let go of his question.

"Dr. Brenda, when are you gonna talk about justice?"

The thing about a good question is that it not only makes you look within; it also makes you look around. As I continued to reflect on that young grad student's question, I also reflected deeply on the ways the world was changing. In 2008, Barack Obama ascended to the highest office in the land and was elected the first African American president of the United States of America. Eight years later, Hillary Rodham Clinton made history by being the first woman to be nominated for president by a major political party.

This historic change in the demographic leadership of the United States did not, however, come without fierce opposition and backlash. A strong and vocal anti-immigration, anti-trade, racially divisive, "law and order" populist sentiment emerged in the American mainstream in the years following President Obama's election and resulted in the election of a known misogynist, bully, and right-wing racist sympathizer, someone who mocked disabled people, villainized any group seen as "other," and encouraged violence—yet was supported by many conservative Christians. Hate crimes are on the rise. Black people worshiping in churches and Jewish people in synagogues are massacred. Young people march through college campuses carrying torches and spewing racism. Brown children are mercilessly ripped from the arms of their parents and kept in cages. This is the world around us—and the church largely remains silent.

Battles that we thought had been fought and won long ago are resurfacing. Rights we once thought secure are now in jeopardy. I, along with others, find myself in constant disbelief at decisions being made, actions being taken, and words being spoken by those in the highest levels of our government.

The seminary student's question started to expand in my mind: *Dr. Brenda, when is the church going to talk about justice?*

How will the belief in God's reconciling work in the world practically impact impoverished people and those discriminated against on the basis of their race, gender, sexuality, class, or social status? How does our belief in the reconciling power of the resurrection of Christ enable us to speak truth against the powers of injustice that are at work in the world? If we can't answer those questions, then we are not relevant and our message of reconciliation is shallow.

If we don't grapple with those issues, then we face the real possibility of losing our credibility because the church and Christians will no longer be important in a culture that is asking different and more pressing questions of those who follow Jesus.

Now more than ever, those who care about the reconciliation command of the cross must speak up and out about injustice and must go about the work of dismantling the structures of this injustice and combating the harmful, even deadly result of this country's unchecked legacy of systemic inequality and discrimination. The church *must* talk about justice. I *must* talk about justice. The time is now.

This was no more apparent to me than in the days, weeks, and months following the horrific death of Michael Brown at the hands of police in Ferguson, Missouri. This was in 2014. The Black Lives Matter movement was in its infancy, and in the wake of this senseless act of violence against a black man, support was galvanizing.

I traveled to Ferguson to meet with a group of thirty to forty evangelical leaders for a faith roundtable following Brown's death. We were there to learn about how the church might respond to the events in Ferguson and the Black Lives Matter movement that was just starting to take shape. We spent several days learning, sharing, strategizing, and imagining the various ways that we could guide the church and the country in the process of healing and reconciliation. While we were there, we visited the headquarters of a prominent group of young activists called Ferguson Action.

The church leaders in the delegation felt excited to meet the activists, to listen, and perhaps to share our wisdom and experience. The young activists, however, were not so interested in hearing about our past experiences; rather, they were focused on what we were planning to do now and in the future. They criticized the church and Christian leaders for our lack of engagement. They criticized the church for its misogyny, its hypocrisy, its complacency, its inactivity, its silence in the face of injustice, and its lack of inclusivity. They believed that the church worked harder to keep people *out* than to invite folks *in*, and they saw no need for the church in the work they were doing.

If they were speaking for their generation, it was abundantly clear that their generation could not care less about what the church has to say. They represented a growing group of people known by sociologists as either the Nones (those with no religious affiliation) or the Dones (those who were once churchgoers and have since left the church but have not abandoned their faith). For both the Nones and the Dones, the church has lost its credibility. These folks aren't waiting for the church, and they aren't expecting Christians to show up. They are only concerned with what the church is willing to do.

They were not being rhetorical or hypothetical. The next day we received a text message from them informing us that there was a protest planned for later that day. The pastor who received the message read it aloud for all of us to hear: "We are meeting on the steps of the municipal court building at 4:00 this afternoon. Are you coming or not?" On the spot, in that moment, I had a decision to make. I had to decide whether my message of reconciliation was going to be only words. I came to convene, not to march. I was not prepared—mentally, spiritually, or physically—to participate in a protest. But there I was. What was I going to do?

The Journey to Bravery

To understand my evolution as a reconciliation leader, you must first understand that I began my journey sincerely believing that if I could convince evangelical Christians that reconciliation was not some politically motivated agenda but a biblical calling rooted in Scripture, they would pursue racial justice. For years I tried to be biblical enough, nonthreatening enough, patient enough, persuasive enough, theologically rigorous enough, so that no one could say I had a hidden agenda. I wanted to see a revival come to and through the church by helping Christians become more actively involved in changing the world through the ministry of reconciliation.

And that's what my ministry was about for a very long time. I preached the good news of multiculturalism and diversity at churches and conferences. I led workshops and taught seminars and told people about inclusion and equity and how Jesus demonstrated these principles in his ministry. But along the way, there were indicators that my approach, while good and well-intentioned, was not effecting the type of change I knew in my heart needed to take place.

As I have continued to wrestle with making sense of what is happening in the world around me, another question has emerged: *What are you going to do about it?* The answer is clear in my spirit, but not easy to fully accept. I decided to become brave—to say the things that I must say and to stand for the truth, regardless of the consequences. I knew that I had to start preaching a more honest and direct message about how we, the church, must work to repair broken systems, alongside those affected by them, in order to engage in reconciliation.

Up until this point, my reconciliation work has been deeply concerned with how my message will be received by white people. I have tried to ensure that offense did not interfere with my message of diversity and harmony. I made my message easy for them to hear. But no more. I have come to realize that over the years, I was used by white-dominant culture, probably not maliciously or intentionally, but unconsciously, to make the conversation about racial reconciliation more palatable, understandable, and acceptable to them. But in the aftermath of the 2016 presidential election, with the white supremacy that evidenced itself in insidious and subtle ways, I made up my mind to no longer be used in this way. I will no longer preach, teach, or lead reconciliation on white-dominant culture's terms.

I have chosen to always remember and affirm that my truth, my spirituality, and my identity are rooted in the black community that raised me, nurtured me, and taught me to fight for a better world where all people can thrive. I am anchored and compelled by this faith that understands what it is to seek justice, equality, and peace.

Now, more than ever, we must all respond to the call of justice. Answering this call requires bravery, which is courage that is developed over time. Looking through the lens of the biblical narrative of Esther, we will reflect on the journey to bravery, both Esther's and my own. In addition to sharing stories, I will share concrete strategies for answering God's call and bravely acting on it. Reconciliation is an ongoing spiritual process involving forgiveness, repentance, and justice; its goal is to transform broken relationships and systems so that they better reflect God's original intention for all creation to flourish. Since this work is an ongoing, transformative process, I myself am becoming braver as I inspire and empower the next generation of reconciliation leaders to repair broken systems so that all people can thrive and reach their full, God-given potential. Therefore, this book is a rallying cry, challenging all of us to find the courage to pursue racial justice by taking big and small risks to get involved now. This is how we grow into the courageous people we want to be—people who find our voice, speak our truth, and stand up for the things we believe in, regardless of the consequences.

So as I write this book, and as you read it, I am praying for you to be brave. I believe that, like Esther, we are in a time that demands our leadership. We are in a time that demands social activism—specifically, social activism from a Christian perspective. I am convinced that we can no longer preach Jesus without justice. Therefore, we must ask ourselves, What is it that Christians can uniquely bring to the table? What does it mean to be Christian activists? We need look no further than the incarnation of Jesus for the answer. Jesus *literally* came and showed up. He showed up to the messy, frightening, beautiful community in which he was born, and he embodied love with his actions and his words. He wasn't indifferent. He wasn't numb to it all. He was present. This is what we are called to do as well. Just like Jesus, we are called to demonstrate our active participation in local, community concerns and relevant social issues. This calling is what we will explore in this book. We will look at how Christ-followers can show up in the world and set about restoring broken systems together with others.

This is what that young man in my seminar was asking me. He wanted to know whether the reconciliation I was preaching required social action that is rooted in a commitment to justice. And now I know the answer is a resounding "Yes!" Reconciliation requires action, and it must be contextual, social, and political. Meeting with those young activists in Ferguson strengthened my resolve and helped me realize that the church has work to do if we are going to regain our credibility with the larger culture. That's why we must redefine and reclaim the reconciliation movement within a larger context to be fully engaged, as Christians, on the social, political, and cultural level.

Esther's influence has both resonance and relevance for the church today. As we move further into her story, we will explore how this young woman is a prototype for Christian activism and an example of reparative reconciliation. We'll explore the ways in which her story demonstrates God's desire to use each and every one of us to advance righteousness and justice, regardless of our social status or leadership development. Her story gives us a unique look into what it means to be involved in social and political activism in order to repair broken systems together.

ONE

THE LAW OF TIMING

I DIDN'T GO looking for reconciliation—the call to racial reconciliation found me. I was a seminary intern at Occidental College, working as an assistant chaplain. When I arrived at Oxy, as we called it, I thought my ministry was going to be focused on women. But then I went to chapel for the first time and noticed that out of the two hundred or so students attending chapel, only two were students of color. There was a black male student who, I later found out, was dating a white woman in the fellowship. The other undergraduate, I learned, was a young man who was Mexican but seemed to distance himself from his ethnic and cultural background.

That experience made me think about my days as a college student at Rutgers University. Trying to be a good Christian, I had visited InterVarsity Christian Fellowship and Campus Crusade for Christ meetings. But I was usually one of only a few black students. Consequently, none of the songs were familiar to me, and I always felt out of place. I remember one occasion when everyone was invited to pray during one of these gatherings. I closed my eyes and began to pray fervently, the way I was accustomed to in my local church. At some point, I noticed that nobody was praying but me, so I opened my eyes only to discover that everybody else was looking at me as if I were from another planet! After that experience, I never went back. Instead, I began attending a Bible study led by African American students in my dormitory.

So, on my first visit to the chapel service at Oxy, I felt the same dynamics at play that I had experienced at Rutgers. It felt like so many things had changed for the church, except in the area of racial reconciliation among Christians. This observation caused me to ask a pressing question that led me into a ministry of racial reconciliation: Why is it so hard for Christians to make any real, significant progress in dealing with the issue of race?

In an attempt to find an answer to that question, I started an ethnic-specific ministry for students of color at Occidental College. I realized that although the existing campus ministries offered valuable Bible study tools and resources, my students needed to have these things "translated" to make them relevant to their life experiences and ways of engaging God. I also noticed that students of color were not being chosen for leadership positions. In order for them to have opportunities to be leaders, I needed to give students of color alternative means to exercise their leadership gifts. I was trying to help them resist the pull toward white-dominant culture by giving them ministry opportunities that would allow them to use their gifts and find their voice in both spiritually and culturally relevant ways. I wanted to help them reclaim their connection to their culture while not losing the new things they had discovered about Jesus through their campus fellowship. Although I didn't realize it at the time, this was the beginning of a new ministry for me: a focus not on women but on racial justice, equity, and ultimately reconciliation.

Looking back over my own life and how my experience as an African American college student uniquely prepared me for a ministry of racial reconciliation on a college campus years later, I can see that it was not by happenstance. Neither was it happenstance that the forty-fourth president of the United States was biracial and spent much of his childhood in the care of his white grandparents. President Barack Obama grew up across America and around the world, in Hawaii, Indonesia, and Boston. A son of Africa and a graduate of Harvard, he earned his stripes on the South Side of Chicago. Throughout his life, Obama was exposed to a broad cross-section of cultures and traditions from an intimate, first-person perspective, not a distant, dispassionate one. He didn't read about it; he lived it. Obama embodies in his personal history and genetic constitution the very requirements of racial and ethnic transcendence that are needed in this new era. I believe that there were certain circumstantial, environmental, and personal elements that coalesced into a perfect storm of conditions that made President Obama's historic election possible. Obama's history and personal life made him the "right" man, which, when met with the state of the nation and the world, made it the "right" time. And the rest, as they say, is history.

To study Obama's presidency is to see a wonderful example of what John Maxwell calls "the law of timing" in his book *The 21 Irrefutable Laws of Leadership*.[1] According to Maxwell, sometimes even when someone is not looking for leadership, when leadership is neither desired nor aspired to, an individual can find herself in a place where God needs her, whether she feels like it or not; whether she wants it or not, the times demand her leadership. While Barack Obama did have hopes of making it to the White House, it wasn't until his hugely popular speech at the Democratic National Convention in 2004 that those hopes started to take a more solid shape and the presidency began to look possible. The timing was right, and when the opportunity presented itself, Obama was ready.

This law of timing offers a very different perspective from the commonly held belief that leaders are born. All of us have undoubtedly heard it said that someone is a "natural-born leader." This expression suggests that there are certain inalienable characteristics a leader manifests that indicate his or her qualification to lead, and either you have those qualities or you don't. The problem with this theory of leadership is that it discounts so many individuals who have tremendous leadership potential and have value to add to society but who, because they may not have been endued with certain gifts from birth, are disqualified before they even get a chance.

I agree with Maxwell and contradict the theory of leadership that relies solely on a person's possession of certain inalienable characteristics. Instead, I believe that a combination of factors produce leadership in a person's life. These factors can certainly include innate gifts, skills, talents, and abilities, but there are also situations that cultivate leadership in individuals who may not otherwise consider themselves to be leaders. And there are circumstances that arrange and present themselves in the lives of individuals to create unique leadership opportunities. I consider this to be the appointed time.

The appointed time can perhaps best be understood as a time when the circumstances of life are so mammoth as to be beyond the control of the individual yet are sufficiently intimate to require or even demand a response from the individual, one that only he or she can provide. Because of both the circumstances (regardless of whether the person wanted them) and the individual's unique suitedness to respond (regardless of whether the person deems herself ready), the individual is thrust into leadership. I believe Obama's presidency happened at an appointed time. The same could be said about the ascendency of other leaders throughout history

Consider Martin Luther King Jr. He did not plan to lead the civil rights movement, but when the movement needed a name and a spokesperson, Reverend King responded. The world was never the same. You may not be familiar with the entire story, but it began on December 1, 1955, when a woman named Rosa Parks refused to give up her seat on a bus in Montgomery, Alabama. Community activists needed a place to hold a meeting to plan the response, a proposed bus boycott, so they asked a young local minister for the use of his church to discuss the matter. That minister was Martin Luther King Jr.

The community members met and agreed to a one-day boycott, which was so successful that they later agreed to extend the boycott. The Montgomery Improvement Association (MIA) was formed to run the boycott, and King was asked to lead the organization. By some accounts, King was initially reluctant, although he planned to support the boycott. He probably had many valid reasons for why he shouldn't be the leader of that burgeoning movement—he was a pastor, a husband, a father of a baby daughter, and an intellectual who wanted to write books. But his proponents were not dissuaded. He seemed "perfect" for the job; he had the "right" education, the "right" background, and the "right" skills. It seemed to them that he was prepared in advance for the position. It was a divine appointment, they thought, and King was eventually persuaded.

It has been said that King was a reluctant leader. History indicates that he did not seek the limelight or fame, but he was one for whom God's divine call could not be ignored. Did he possess innate leadership qualities? Certainly. He was well-spoken, educated, and passionate about the plight of his people, but I also believe that King understood the meaning of the God-ordained moment. King was prepared by experiences, cultivated by his education, and endowed with certain personality traits and characteristics that made him the ideal person to lead a national movement at that precise moment in time.

The MIA successfully ran the Montgomery bus boycott for a historic 381 days. The boycott thrust King into the national spotlight as a civil rights leader. All because he agreed to let a group of community leaders hold a meeting in his church. I imagine that he agreed to serve, agreed to lead the bus boycott, without knowing that it would eventually morph into leading the modern-day civil rights movement.

Most of us don't think of ourselves as activists. In the face of enormous global and national issues, we can feel numb. I read the headlines, and you know what I want to do sometimes? I want to get back in bed and pull the covers over my head. I'm guessing that many of you may feel the same way. It's simply too much! We just want to get the kids to school, go to work, find a job, get an education, and make it through the day. But I would argue that, as Christians, whether we feel ready or qualified, we are *all* called to be activists.

King was an unlikely activist—so was Esther. She was a young woman who was reluctant to step into the spotlight. She didn't see herself as a leader, and she certainly wasn't seeking to be an activist. In fact, when her cousin Mordecai approached her to intervene on behalf of her people, her first response was, "Who, *me?*"

As we saw earlier, both King and Obama were presented with opportunities to lead, and both had to make a decision; both had to willingly and knowingly assent to the call to leadership. No doubt at some point along the decision-making process, or perhaps even in the early days of walking in leadership, both men wrestled with their own qualifications to lead. There were undoubtedly moments when they wondered whether they were in fact uniquely suited to face the circumstances in which they found themselves. I imagine there were times when their minds swirled with questions and when they asked themselves, with great angst, "Who, *me?*"

You may be reading this book thinking the same kinds of thoughts. *You want me to lead a movement of racial reconciliation on my campus?* Or, *You want me to start a new racial reconciliation ministry at my church?* Or, *You want me to share my experience?* Or, *You want me to stand up for justice in my community?* You may be wondering whether

33

you have what it takes. You may, in fact, be asking yourself the very same question likely asked by Obama and King and every other leader who answered God's call to leadership at one time or another: "Who, *me*?"

I answer your question with a resounding, "Yes, *you*!"

If you are reading this book, you are precisely the right person to accomplish whatever God is asking of you right now. I would encourage you by saying that the task before you, however monumental it may seem in your eyes, is not too big for God. I would go even further and assert that you have been uniquely prepared to take on this new leadership responsibility, whatever it is. I would tell you that your history, your education (formal or informal), and your experience are all coming together in this moment to enable you to accomplish what is being asked of you. You were made for this moment. You are on this earth, in this moment, in your community, to be a voice, a beacon, a light for such a time as this.

However, just because it may be your appointed time does not mean that saying yes to the call of leadership comes easily. It seems that every great leader endures a time of questioning or doubt. Esther was no different, and neither are we. Esther had fears. Mordecai had to convince her that perhaps she was sent to the palace for this very moment, for the very crisis that was before her. Mordecai let her know that it was her God-appointed time. Esther answered the call of God on her life and, in so doing, also answered her own question of "Who, *me*?" with a resounding "Yes!"

TWO

THE MAKING OF AN ACTIVIST

Mordecai had a very beautiful cousin named Esther, whose Hebrew name was Hadassah. He had raised her as his own daughter, after her father and mother died. When the king ordered the search for beautiful women, many were taken to the king's palace in Susa, and Esther was one of them.

Esther 2:7–8

I BECAME A CHRISTIAN at age nineteen and was nurtured in the Black Pentecostal church tradition. I honor that experience as the foundation of my faith, but I also admit that we had a conservative isolationism that did not prepare me to be socially active. The basic message I heard was to "come out from the world" and devote myself to the safety and sanctity of the church. That's why I was encouraged to avoid anything considered to be "worldly," including secular music. As a result, only Christian radio or television programs were okay for me to consume. I didn't realize it at the time, but the Christian message of Jesus Christ was woven into a social, political, and cultural worldview of white supremacy that was unduly influencing me.

So, although it is hard for me to admit, when I was in college I voted for Ronald Reagan. President Jimmy Carter was running for reelection, and in retrospect I believe he was the most devout, evangelical, churchgoing, Sunday school–teaching Christian who ever served as president of the United States. But Carter only served one term because conservative Christians on those radio and television programs I had listened to unified to get him out of office. He came under fire from the religious right because of the new IRS rules revoking the tax-exempt status of racially segregated private Christian schools. Many Christian colleges and universities had written or spoken policies against interracial dating and marriage, and they resented this interference into their affairs. So when Carter's opponent in the general election was Reagan, most born-again Christians fully supported the Republican. Reagan ran as a staunch fiscal conservative and a Cold War hawk who promised steep increases in military spending. Reagan accused his opponent of failing to confront the Soviet Union when he signed the Strategic Arms Limitation Treaty (SALT II) in an effort to establish numerical equality between the superpowers in their nuclear weapons delivery systems. Somehow, the televangelists I was listening to explained this as a form of collusion with the antichrist.

I was a young Christian, and the message that came across loud and clear was, "If you are a good, Bible-believing Christian, you won't vote for Jimmy Carter." That form of right-wing indoctrination worked on me, and I voted for Reagan. I didn't understand it then, but I came to see that when I was listening to their Bible studies and worship songs, I was also buying into their white ideology and worldview. This was one of the most pivotal turning points in my life. After that vote, I made up my mind that I would *never again* let white evangelicals tell me how to think or vote. White evangelicals will co-opt people of color's understanding of Scripture, as well as how we understand the social and political world around us. That's why I vowed to scrutinize everything for myself, to find alternative news sources, and to become more informed about what is happening to people who are experiencing real life-and-death situations.

Years later, when my husband and I moved to Chicago, I paid careful attention to what happened to Laquan McDonald, a young African American man who was shot sixteen times within thirteen seconds by a white officer. The Chicago Police Department held on to the tape of the shooting for over a year before releasing it to the public. In November 2015, hundreds of Chicago pastors, religious leaders, and other community members marched on police headquarters in Chicago to protest. By the time of the clergy members' protest, the city had been in a state of unrest for more than a week. Pastor Charlie Dates of Progressive Baptist Church told local media, "I think it's the church's responsibility to call for justice. There are many people calling for justice tonight all over America. However, ours is undergirded with a call for righteousness."[1]

The clergy in attendance were rising up with impassioned prayers, speeches, and rallying cries. It was truly a group effort by pastors throughout Chicago who wished to see systemic change in their city. The religious leaders also organized a time of prayer in front of police headquarters, and at one point in the evening someone passed the megaphone to the young pastor of River City Community Church, Daniel Hill. Daniel is a dear friend of mine, and I know that he didn't see himself as an activist. He was just there as one of literally hundreds of other pastors and religious leaders. He saw himself as an ordinary guy—a pastor, a family man, a concerned community member. But when one of the other pastors asked him to pray in the midst of their gathering, Daniel stepped up and called white Christians like himself to repent for failing to value Black lives.

It is this very call to understand whiteness and Daniel Hill's simple prayer of white repentance that represents the heart of the new paradigm for racial reconciliation. We must take the problem of whiteness more seriously in order to help churches become racially transformed communities of justice and equality. For reconciliation to accomplish its true goal, it is critical to understand whiteness as a social construct created to divide racial groups and assert the superiority of one group over others. The concept of race was developed as a way of categorizing, labeling, and separating human beings on the basis of their physical characteristics, such as hair texture, head shape, and skin color. This ideology produced the social constructs of white supremacy that justified the enslavement, dehumanization, exploitation, and annihilation of human beings who were not Europeans. I agree with author Ta-Nehisi Coates when he observes in his book *Between the World and Me* that "the people who believe themselves to be white . . . have created a social system that assumes everything belongs to them and they have a right to do anything. This has led to catastrophic consequences for people all over the world because as James Baldwin said, '[They] have brought humanity to the edge of oblivion: because they think they are white.'"[2]

Whiteness is a human construction, created for and by white people. Being white is not a sin in and of itself. But "whiteness"—the elevation and valuation of those who are white above all other racial groups, and the systems and structures that support this elevation—is evil. Regrettably, many of our white brothers and sisters in Christ are, consciously or unconsciously, complicit in this evil of racial injustice. In an interview published as "What Does Repentance Look Like for the White Church?" writer, speaker, and activist Lisa Sharon Harper says,

> We have done two things for too long. One, we have centered white people in our conversations around race and power. We have placed at the center of the conversation the question of whether or not white people will accept the message. . . . Second, we have spent too much time centering our attention on winning the hearts and minds of white people rather than focusing on our own communities. Not in a way that gives charity or exercises compassionate ministries, but in a way that changes the power equations in our districts, our municipalities, our cities, our states and our nations.[3]

Daniel Hill didn't realize it in that moment at the protest, but his words presented an alternative to mere relational proximity, shining a light on the systemic inequalities that he, as a white man, and his white sisters and brothers have accepted, tolerated, or ignored at a cost significant to the

Black community. The new paradigm he was articulating represented such a radical change that the world took notice. His prayer led to significant media coverage, including magazine articles, internet news features, and a television interview on CNN. It was truly a wild ride for the young pastor. The current social climate of police brutality and cover-ups in the United States created a calling for unlikely leaders, such as Reverend Hill, to step up and become social activists. He didn't wake up that morning thinking he was going to do something great. He simply stepped up to the megaphone when it was offered and spoke out of his years of experience as a pastor of a multiethnic church in the city of Chicago. When the opportunity presented itself to speak up for justice, Hill was ready.

It wasn't all rosy after that night. Hill was attacked on social media, his and his family's safety was threatened, his church had to hire security—all of which quickly demonstrated that there is a price for taking a stand. Racial hatred came out of the woodwork after that one seemingly insignificant prayer. White Christians attacked Hill on nearly every front. It was truly astounding to witness the extent of the racial hatred that was leveled at him. He had no idea that it would be so vile and so potentially violent and soon came to realize the amount of courage he would be called to if he chose to continue fighting for justice, accountability, and racial reconciliation in Chicago. He also came to understand and appreciate in a new way the sacrifices and bravery of those who had gone before him, fighting so valiantly, long before he even arrived on the scene.

We see the same thing play out in the book of Esther: she also was not looking to be an activist. When we are first introduced to Esther, her name is actually Hadassah. Just your average young person living in Persia, she probably wasn't thinking about influencing anyone, let alone standing up for justice. She was likely about sixteen years old, and we know only a few things about her. First, we know that she was pretty. When we meet her in Esther 2:7, we're told that she was lovely—so lovely, in fact, that she was one of the women selected to stand before King Xerxes after he banished Queen Vashti, which we will discuss in the next chapter. Being beautiful and young likely meant that Esther was focused on one thing and one thing only: getting married and securing her future. She was probably like any other normal teenager. She had goals and aspirations. Maybe she had a boyfriend or someone she was fond of. Perhaps she dreamed of the day that she would get married, have children, and raise a family of her own so she could finally have a normal life. Maybe living a "normal" life was what she most longed for, since she had already experienced great anguish in her young life.

Hadassah had endured some real-life struggles. She was the unfortunate bearer of both personal and emotional pain. Her mother and father were both dead, and she was being raised by a cousin. Both my mom and my dad have passed away, and I know from my own experience that there is a distinct and profound trauma to being in the world without your parents. It's different from losing other members of your family. Something about it causes you to feel uniquely alone, and Hadassah was just a child when it happened to her. We can surmise, although the text doesn't tell us explicitly, that this loss must have resulted in all manner of abandonment, trust, and intimacy issues for her. It's safe to say that all of us experience loss and the accompanying emotional trauma in similar ways. Whatever the loss—whether getting a divorce or being fired, or perhaps losing a friend, a sibling, a child, or a parent—we all know on some level what it must have felt like to be Hadassah: alone, disillusioned, frightened, and frustrated.

Hadassah was an orphan being raised by her cousin Mordecai. This tells us even more about her. It was uncommon to be raised by a single male in that day and age, so we know by default that Hadassah literally had no one else. I have always wondered: Where were the women in her family who should have taken in this young girl and shown her how to care for herself as a female? We can only surmise that she had no aunties to raise her, no grandmother, no older sisters. She was utterly and completely alone in the world except for this one cousin. Can you imagine?

We also know that Hadassah was not well-off or of high status in her community. She was an orphan living in a single-guardian home. And on top of that, she was a Jew, and the Jews were exiles in Persia. She was an immigrant, living in a foreign land. She was at the bottom of the social ladder, just an ordinary teenager trying to figure out her future. Being an activist was likely the furthest thing from her mind when she comes into view in the opening chapters of the book of Esther. She was a young woman with modest hopes and dreams who had been through some of life's greatest hardships already in her young life. In the words of the iconic poem by legendary poet Langston Hughes, titled "Mother to Son," life for Hadassah "ain't been no crystal stair."[4]

For all that we know about Esther, there's also a lot that we don't know. The Bible leaves out a lot of details. For example, we don't know how her parents died. We don't know what happened to the rest of her family, although it's probably safe to assume that they were dead as well. We don't know much about Mordecai, this cousin who was raising her, except that he was a Benjamite who had been among the captives carried away from Jerusalem by King Nebuchadnezzar of Babylon. Don't you want to know more about her? I sure do! I want to know more of the facts. I want to know so much more about young Hadassah and how she got in this situation. But the Bible doesn't tell us. Why not?

I think the Bible leaves out many of the specific details on purpose. As much as I want the full rundown, the silence of the text is important. We want the details and the information on Hadassah because that is how we try to understand who people are and attempt to make sense of their situation. This information helps us decide whether we can empathize with people, whether we think they deserve to be in that situation, and so on. We like to categorize and organize people into subsets and easily understandable groups: young, old, pretty, plain, powerful, uneducated, intellectual, homeless, lazy. It's normal. Everybody does it. But perhaps it's for this very reason that the text leaves out so many details about our young heroine. If we knew more about her, we might discount who she was. We might be tempted to disqualify her. But God doesn't want us to do that! God doesn't want us to categorize or disqualify Hadassah, and God doesn't want us to categorize or disqualify ourselves because of the parts of our story that make us feel "less than" or "other"— parts of our story such as depression, addiction, divorce, unemployment, wayward children, or any manner of defeat and disappointment.

Some of us may doubt our capacity to be used by God because of the painful experiences that have taken place in our lives. But I want to let you know that it doesn't matter where you start in life, what side of the tracks you come from, or how different your family may be. The fact that you may have had a difficult beginning does not disqualify you from being a leader. Your potential is not determined by the home that you came from. The fact that there's been some drama in your life doesn't limit your capacity to be used by God. You may be young or inexperienced like Hadassah, but do not disqualify yourself from leading because of your age, gender, or the difficult circumstances you may have experienced in life. You're not disqualified from being used as a leader, an agent of change!

It's important that we not disqualify ourselves for this reason: our limitations and shortcomings do not limit the power of God to transform and redeem our lives for good. We all have areas of brokenness in our lives, and God is still able to use us to help others. To acknowledge our weaknesses gives an authenticity and humility to our leadership that others can relate to and identify with. Brené Brown, a scholar on vulnerability and best-selling author of the book *Rising Strong*, says, "The irony is that we attempt to disown our difficult stories to appear more whole or more acceptable, but our wholeness—even our wholeheartedness—actually depends on the integration of all our experiences, including the falls."[5] Therefore, when we disqualify ourselves or others, we deny the possibility of God intervening in our human stories and transforming our situations in miraculous ways.

The specifics? The details? These particular aspects of our stories are not what's most important. All of these things shape us, but they don't have the power to derail God's purposes. What really matters is that, when the time arose, Hadassah stepped up and became the activist God was calling her to be. What matters is that, when someone asked Daniel Hill to pray that day, he was ready. What matters is that, when the civil rights of ordinary people were denied, they marched and refused to ride buses. This is what the story of Esther is all about. It's about unlikely leaders and unlikely activists sensing the call of God on their lives and being ready and willing to step forward.

Although I had been working in racial reconciliation for years, I felt like an unlikely activist that day in Ferguson too. I felt uncertain about my role in this movement. I felt that in many ways the movement was for the younger generation, not for me. I traveled to Ferguson to learn, listen, advise, and consult; I was not ready to actively participate. But there I was—standing awestruck as a young brother opened the trunk of his car to reveal the supplies necessary for a protest, including a gas mask and bottles of water (to clear one's eyes from tear gas). My head was spinning as he reminded me to leave my purse in the trunk but to take my ID. I couldn't believe how ill-equipped and unprepared I was for this moment.

Still, I forged ahead into the throng of protestors. I raised my hands and lifted my voice and joined the others who had gathered there with the intention of proclaiming and protecting the humanity of black lives and black bodies. I was invigorated by the energy of the crowd, but as the protest progressed, I started to become a little nervous as some of the young people became more agitated. One young white man started to shake the barricades that had been erected by the police to prevent the protestors from approaching the city hall administrative building.

The more the barriers shook, the more nervous I became. I looked around to see whether anyone else joined me in my growing trepidation, but everyone else seemed lost in the momentum of the movement, and the energy kept rising. The protest remained peaceful, but it seemed to me that the police were standing just a little closer than they had been only a few moments before. My attention shifted back to the young protestor who was rattling the barricades and was joined now by a few others, becoming more animated.

I didn't know what to do, and no one else seemed to be bothered. I had enough experience to know all the terrible things that could happen, and the militarized police response in Ferguson was already well-documented. I truly felt that all of our lives were potentially in danger. I knew, though, that God was calling me there for this moment. I stood still for a moment, until I felt an unction in my spirit to kneel and pray. And so that's what I did. In the middle of the street and in the midst of the yelling and screaming, I started to pray.

I am not sure what I expected to happen. Perhaps I was envisioning some sort of mass genuflection, like what I'd seen in the movie *Selma*. But that didn't happen. I remained kneeling in prayer while what appeared to be chaos broke out all around me. Folks were chanting and screaming, and the barriers kept rattling. As I stood up from my prayer, my eyes full and my cheeks wet with tears, a young woman, wearing a red cap, was scurrying by. When she saw me crying, she took my hand in hers. I wasn't sure what was about to happen, but she squeezed my hand into a fist and raised our hands as one into the air, shouting, "From Palestine to Ferguson!" Then she ran off.

I was struck by her sense of connection between the struggle for the liberation of Palestinians in Israel and the liberation of black people in America. For me, it made the entire moment incredibly personal. It helped me realize that just as the Laquan McDonalds and the Michael Browns of our time have galvanized movements of liberation, so it is that diverse and seemingly disparate individuals such as myself and the young Palestinian woman, by joining together under the umbrella of a common understanding of humanity, can make a difference.

THREE

WHAT CALLED YOU FORTH?

King Xerxes of Persia lived in his capital city of Susa and ruled one hundred twenty-seven provinces from India to Ethiopia. During the third year of his rule, Xerxes gave a big dinner for all his officials and officers. . . .

While the men were enjoying themselves, Queen Vashti gave the women a big dinner inside the royal palace.

By the seventh day, King Xerxes was feeling happy because of so much wine. And he asked his seven personal servants, Mehuman, Biztha, Harbona, Bigtha, Abagtha, Zethar, and Carkas, to bring Queen Vashti to him. The king wanted her to wear her crown and let his people and his officials see how beautiful she was. The king's servants told Queen Vashti what he had said.

Esther 1:1–3, 9–12

ONE DAY I was on a plane headed to preach and was reading the book *Dear White Christians* by Jennifer Harvey.[1] I came across a section in which she was critiquing leaders who have been active in the reconciliation movement. She argued that they had unwittingly reduced the message of reconciliation to one of diversity and inclusion by not insisting on justice. I found myself nodding in agreement with her.

According to Harvey, the reconciliation movement was rooted in the precept that as long as we had multicultural and multiethnic churches, we had achieved the goal of reconciliation. She challenged the long-held belief that reconciliation in the church simply means celebrating everyone's culture. She went on to list several reconciliation leaders as being culpable in perpetuating this paradigm. I kept nodding and reading—until I turned to the page where she named me.

I was stunned. But deep down, I knew Harvey was right. I knew that the relational, diversity-oriented approach to reconciliation had grown stale and was not leading to real, lasting change. I agreed, and still agree, with her conclusion that this message of reconciliation is not able to produce real social change because it is too rooted in a narrative about coming together across our various differences. The previous message was more palatable to white Christians because it did not focus on or demand justice from them. Instead, it implied that white Christians and Christians of color have parallel work to do in order to repair racial brokenness. But as Harvey points out, this approach does not take seriously the realities, both historic and current, that produced and continue to uphold divisiveness, nor does it acknowledge the specific work that different groups must do to repair the divide. On the flight that day, I sensed that something was calling me forth to engage reconciliation in a radically new way.

Discerning the Times

This reminds me of a profound West African concept that is expressed in the form of a question. The Akan people in Ghana believe that all people are born with purpose and destiny written into their being. The Akan are monotheistic and believe that no one is here on earth by accident. There is a reason why the God of the universe has summoned every human being to be born. Therefore, according to traditional custom of the Akan people, when someone wants to know a person better, they ask them the following powerful and prophetic question: "What called you forth?"

In asking this question they are essentially asking the person to discuss why they believe they were born. Perhaps the name they were given by their parents holds some insight into what they view as their purpose in life. By asking "What called you forth?" they are really interested in knowing, Why did God cause you to be born at this time in history? Do you know your purpose for being on the planet? What is happening in the world today that called you forth?

As a young girl of fourteen or fifteen, Esther had no idea that what was happening in the sociopolitical world around her would call her forth and have a direct impact on her life. She was likely unaware of what was taking place in Susa, the center of political, legislative, economic, and judicial power in the Persian Empire during the fifth century BCE. She wasn't up on the news coming out of the capital. It wouldn't have been relevant to her. She probably didn't even know that the king, Xerxes, was throwing the most lavish party you could imagine in that hotbed of political clout.

That's how the book of Esther begins. It opens with a lavish party in the city of Susa. And I'm not talking about your basic birthday party or bar mitzvah. This was a party to *end* all parties. It was a party that went on for seven days. Can you imagine?

Before the party even started, King Xerxes invited the armies of Persia to spend 180 days in the capital. This was a chance for the king to show all the people under his reign just how powerful he was. Today we see these kinds of displays by world leaders who launch "test missiles" that aren't really tests at all but rather a chance to show the rest of the world exactly what they are capable of and just how much power they hold over the rest of us. We see it in the synchronized marching of armies through city streets, legs lifting in unison as the sound of their feet pounding the pavement reverberates in the ears of every civilian watching. We saw it in Germany during the rise of Adolf Hitler. When the Nazis came to power, the soldiers and civilian policemen were given license to arbitrarily beat or kill persons they deemed to be opponents, and there was little to no accountability for their violence. This served to incite fear in the people of Europe and around the world. *That's* what King Xerxes was doing when he brought the Persian armies into the capital. He wanted to create an aura of fear and show exactly how much power he held over his people.

After his six-month display of military might, King Xerxes brought in the leaders from his entire empire, along with some rulers from beyond his borders, for this extravagant party to end all parties. He was the king of over 127 provinces, from India to Cush, which stretched from modern-day India all the way to Ethiopia. That's some serious territory!

And this was a serious party. It was the third year of his reign as king, everyone in the capital city of Susa was invited, and it lasted an entire week. It was a veritable who's who of fifth-century (BCE) Persia and a chance for King Xerxes to show off his might in the same fashion we've seen from so many others like him since. Anyone who witnessed the military displays in Susa followed by the over-the-top opulence of this party understood that this was not a person to be trifled with. This man was as powerful as they came, and he was making sure that everybody knew it. It was, in essence, a parade of his political influence and power over the people in his provinces, and it was almost certainly intended to arouse both fear and admiration.

On the one hand, I imagine that the people in his provinces felt significant fear, but I also imagine that they were inspired as well. These demonstrations of power usually provoke as much patriotism as fear, and I'm sure there were many who were ready to join ranks with King Xerxes and follow him to the ends of the earth if it meant they could be part of his entourage.

Those who were in attendance had a chance to throw their lot in with this king and share in a small piece of his power and prestige. Imagine the scene: chefs working day and night to provide all sorts of opulent food and wine, servants cleaning around the clock, entertainment and dancing for days, and all manner of drinking and general merrymaking. The decadence was astounding—all night, all day, nonstop drinking, dancing, eating, entertaining, and sexual promiscuity. And by the time we enter the story in the opening chapter of Esther, everyone has been overindulging and the party is in full swing.

Xerxes was thirty-six when he became king of Persia. According to writer and artist Steven Stuckey, Xerxes was known as a cruel leader who lost a doomed war against the Greeks that his father had started.[2] History remembers him as an impetuous ruler who loved to drink and who abdicated responsibility for decisions made by his advisers on his behalf; they seemed to exist only to tell him what he wanted to hear. It was also said that he married a queen he did not like, which led to his cavorting with a vast harem of beautiful women.

This is important insight into Xerxes as a political leader. Already in the first chapter of Esther we see him violating the scriptural injunction of Proverbs 31:4–5: "It is not for kings to drink wine, not for rulers to crave beer, lest they drink and forget what has been decreed, and deprive all the oppressed of their rights" (NIV). Although his political advisers could see his shortcomings, they were unable to give wise advice when he needed it because Xerxes surrounded himself with seven nobles who were all very much like him. They were all male and wildly insulated, which made them unable to understand the different genders, cultures, and languages around them or give counsel about how the king should lead them.

It's during his ostentatious party when we first hear about Queen Vashti. Is she the one the king didn't want? We don't know. What we do know is that the men were in separate chambers from the women during the partying so that "boys could be boys," partaking of the wine that flowed without restraint and engaging with prostitutes at will. After drinking for days on end, King Xerxes was drunk, and it was at this point that he asked his servants to go and get

Queen Vashti. He wanted to put her on display and show her off to all the men at his party. She was his ultimate prize, and he no doubt wanted them to be amazed by her breathtaking beauty. He wanted to parade her about as his possession and demanded that she come dressed in her full regalia.

But, in a move that was likely unheard of at the time, Vashti refused. After imagining what that party was probably like, I can certainly see why. Although we don't get a lot of information about what Vashti was thinking at this point, if we read between the lines, I imagine her wondering what she is really being asked to do when the advisers ask her to come stand before the king and all his drunken party guests. She certainly would have known that she would have to diminish herself and lose her dignity in order to obey the king's orders. She knew what it would mean to parade in front of this group of men. She was being disrespected by the king and would likely be forced into any manner of sexual activity against her will. She was considered a possession of the king and was expected to come when she was summoned, without question. But put yourself in her shoes for a moment: As a woman, would you have wanted to enter a room full of drunken men who had already been partying for *days*? I definitely wouldn't.

We ultimately know very little about Queen Vashti, but I believe she was the first activist in the book of Esther. In a time when women had absolutely no agency over their own lives, Vashti took a stand. Harriet Beecher Stowe calls Vashti's disobedience the "first stand for women's rights."[3] She listened to her own core values and respectfully declined to enter a room full of lustful men in what would have been considered an outrageous act of civil disobedience. It was an act of protest. What a brave woman! While little is known about her, I believe she had a deep sense of dignity and that she, and perhaps she alone, understood her value and worth as a human. She knew what she was being asked to do, and she would not, *could* not, do it.

She must have known that, the second she stepped foot in the king's presence that night, she would no longer be herself. And so, she chose not to obey.

This reminds me of the life and legacy of Ida B. Wells, one of the most unsung freedom fighters in US history, whose legacy took a back seat to the stories of so many others. Most of us, for example, do not know as much about Ida B. Wells as we do about Rosa Parks, and we will never know as much about Vashti as we do about Esther. But like Wells—the journalist, newspaper editor, suffragist, sociologist, and civil rights activist who was born a slave and went on to lead an anti-lynching crusade in the United States in the 1890s—Vashti deserves a place in the annals of history. Wells's pursuit of justice spurred the Great Migration (when millions of African Americans left the Jim Crow South for the North and Midwest), halted the nationwide epidemic of lynching, and helped birth the NAACP. She was one of the most courageous, prophetic, and influential leaders in our history. Nonetheless, few people even know her name.

So too with Queen Vashti. Both of these women faded into obscurity and never got the full public recognition they well deserved. But it was because of Ida B. Wells that Rosa Parks became the mother of the civil rights movement. The same is true of Vashti and Esther. Vashti's civil disobedience paved the way for Esther to enter into the story of God's healing and deliverance for the Jews. It was the courageous sacrifice of Vashti that called Esther forth. Had there not been a Vashti who stood up for herself, there would not have been an Esther.

Vashti's refusal to come to the party *infuriated* King Xerxes. It meant he lost face in front of his comrades. We already know that he wasn't a beloved leader. He was more of a frightening demagogue than anything else, and Vashti threw this back in his face. Her sense of worth and her willingness to stand up for herself irrevocably enraged him. His advisers, likewise, could scarcely believe what Vashti had done. They convinced the king that he needed to make a public example of Vashti lest her actions have far-reaching consequences. They believed that the women throughout his provinces would certainly hear about her refusal to come to the king during the party and might think that they too could refuse to obey their husbands. Not to mention the way that it undermined his authority and the power he had worked so hard to display.

I can't help but wonder how the story might have unfolded if the king had sought the advice of a trusted female adviser. Even if it was culturally impossible for him to consult a woman, perhaps he could have had a private conversation with his mother, for example, or with a sister (if he had one)—someone he could trust not to culturally embarrass him but who could still impart insight from a different gender perspective. We don't know how this might have changed the outcome, but we can at least wonder.

What we do know is that Vashti stood up for herself and, as a result, paid a steep price. Being an activist doesn't necessarily make you a hero. Sometimes it means you will lose it all and must face the consequences alone. That is absolutely what happened to Vashti. She lost *everything*. She was banished from the kingdom; we don't hear her name again. We will never know what happened to her, but I pray and believe that God redeemed her life nonetheless. I picture her walking away from the king with tears streaming down her face for all she's lost but with her back straight and her head held high.

Sometimes I wish I could start a Vashti movement that would hold her up as an example—to all of us—of the importance of knowing our worth as human beings. Through her we see that sometimes the people who say they love us don't know how to value or respect us. That's why we must not compromise our dignity, self-esteem, and self-worth in an attempt to please others, to maintain a relationship, or to keep the peace. Vashti shows us that things can happen that are worse than losing a relationship or a job or being disowned by family members or unfriended on social media. By her brave decision to disobey the king, she demonstrates that we must intrinsically value ourselves because there will be times when the people around us won't know how to value us. So, if you get put out, or if the person you love breaks off the relationship, or if your so-called friends unfriend you because you won't lower your standards, follow Queen Vashti and hold your head up high. Walk away with dignity and respect and give them the royal wave as you leave with your self-esteem intact.

This may sound like a dramatic story, but it's not. Vashti's story, which later becomes Esther's story, is a story of ordinary people. While these two women might seem like unlikely activists, I would argue that we are *all* unlikely activists. Very few of us set out on any given day to stand up for something as strongly as Vashti does. But sometimes something happens in the social and political contexts of our lives, something that collides with our personal lives or our family's life and compels us to take a stand. We see no other way forward. Many of us may be feeling that way today.

That's exactly how I was feeling in Ferguson when the young activists asked me and the other church leaders whether we were going to join them in protest later that day. The social and political times had set the stage so that there was no way forward other than to take a stand. Was it a stand I was willing to take? In that moment, I tried to count the cost. I thought about the possibility of getting arrested. I thought about what would happen with my family if I were detained in Ferguson. I thought about the physical risk of getting teargassed. I considered my reputation, my position, and my stature, and I asked myself whether I was willing to put it all in jeopardy in that moment. Was I ready for my Vashti moment?

There was only one answer I could give, only one response that would align with my preaching and posture on reconciliation—and that answer was a resounding, if slightly reluctant, "Yes." I was compelled to take a stand against the persistent forces that continued to deny the humanity of black and brown bodies as evidenced by the ongoing slaughter of our sons and daughters by the police.

Is there anything happening in the world around you that may be calling you forth? What type of leadership is needed in the social and political climate in which you find yourself?

These are the kinds of questions we must ask ourselves as we seek to accurately discern the times in which we live. As we move forward on the journey to becoming socially active Christians, may we be like the leaders referenced in 1 Chronicles 12:32: "The tribe of Issachar supplied 200 leaders, along with all of their relatives under their command. They kept up-to-date in their understanding of the times and knew what Israel should do" (ISV).

As the church, we can no longer afford to hide behind our gilded and stained-glass walls and wring our hands about what is going on "out there" in the world. No, we must see with new eyes, paying attention to what is happening in the world around us and discerning how God is prompting us to respond. This means looking for signs of where God is actively at work in human affairs. It also involves asking new questions and listening to God and others for answers that help us recognize indications that we are being called forth and cause us to know what we should do.

It is this type of discernment that called Vashti and Esther to come forth. This spiritual practice of learning to understand and accurately interpret what is happening around us is a skill that must be cultivated over time and that is best done with others, like the community that formed in Ferguson. That's why I and the other ministers and spiritual leaders showed up. Why did they have to ask us whether we were going to join them in protest? It should have been a given. The church has lost the respect of the culture at large, particularly that of the younger generation rising up before our eyes; it's time for us to put up or shut up. I sincerely believe that a unique opportunity lies before us as Christians—an opportunity to repent for the ways we have not shown up when the disenfranchised, the hurting, and those who have been treated unfairly desperately needed us to show up. We are being called forth. The only question now is how we are going to respond to that call.

FOUR

WHEN POLITICS
BECOMES PERSONAL

Mordecai had warned Esther not to tell anyone that she was a Jew, and she obeyed him. He was anxious to see how Esther was getting along and to learn what had happened to her. So each day he would walk back and forth in front of the court where the women lived.

Esther 2:10-11

AS AN African American woman, I'm acutely aware that many of us bear the weight of reconciliation in our bodies. This is not some social experiment for us. The call to reconciliation takes a toll on us. It takes something out of us to keep being the weather vane or the canary in the coal mine for the good of the church and the greater society. We feel this with our lives. This is one reason why women of color are dying earlier than our white counterparts are. Usually the story is one of institutional racism, of bearing the stress burdens of resistance—the outcome of our generosity. Yes, we are dying of generosity, of the generous gift of offering ourselves—our bodies, our emotions, our spirits—to people who don't really want it or deserve it and who are often hostile to it. Frequently those people are our brothers and sisters in Christ, and yes, this is devastating.

Unfortunately, our generosity causes us to do this over and over and over again, hoping for different results. Then, when we feel weary and tired and say, "I can't play that role for you anymore. I can't be that person for you. I can't carry this for you. I need you to do your work. Yes, I need *you* to do your work!" we are seen as the ones who have changed. We're no longer a team player. We're not friendly. We're being too political. We no longer care about reconciliation. This has happened repeatedly, and there are numerous stories of the many casualties of war. The moment that women and people of color stand up and talk about reconciliation from our most deeply truthful place—where we name what's really happening and no longer put a smiley face on it—those in the dominant culture find ways to withdraw their support from our ministries. In essence, they find ways to make sure that our voices are not heard, that our books are not read, and that we no longer have access to places of influence. That's how power works! However, truth be told, I don't think those people really understand the burden we have carried and continue to carry for them on behalf of the greater good.

That's what happened to Queen Vashti. With her sudden banishment, King Xerxes found himself alone and depressed.

All of the guests who were invited to his lavish party were now gone. The show was over and there was nobody left to impress. The king realized what he had done in banishing the only woman who had the beauty and regal dignity to be queen. He was in a real bind of needing a new queen to replace Vashti. The entire kingdom was waiting to see who this would be. When his anger with Vashti had sufficiently cooled, the king gathered his political advisers, who seemed to regularly give him poor guidance, and declared that he would be holding a beauty pageant of sorts to replace his former queen. His plan was to gather the most beautiful young women from each of his provinces to come before him so that he could choose the one who pleased him most.

This was not like a beauty pageant that we might envision today, something similar to Miss America or Miss Universe. This pageant was held by forced participation. Here is how the contest worked: Young, beautiful women from each province were taken against their will and brought before Hegai, the castrated male servant in charge of the king's women. The ones who were deemed most beautiful were brought into the palace, where they stayed for an entire year. During that time, they were given servants and beauty treatments that consisted of fragrant oils, choice creams, and rich foods. At the end of the twelve months, each woman was sent in to spend the night with King Xerxes. We can couch it in all sorts of G-rated terms, but we all know what happened to them. Those young girls were sexually exploited, forced to have sex with King Xerxes. Given the cultural practices of that time, they would have all been virgins when they entered his royal bedroom. In the morning, they were sent to the house for secondary wives, the harem, where they waited to receive word of their fate. King Xerxes, after sleeping with each of the girls in turn, would declare one of them the new queen, and the rest would be relegated to the role of concubine.

This reminds me of what happened on the night of April 14, 2014, when 276 female students were kidnapped from the Government Secondary School in the town of Chibok in Borno State, Nigeria. Boko Haram, an extremist and terrorist organization based in northeastern Nigeria, claimed responsibility. In the days and weeks that followed, a massive online campaign known as #BringBackOurGirls was launched with the hope that the groundswell of support worldwide would bring a swift resolution and the girls would be promptly returned.

If you followed the story, you know that it did not fully work. Although many of the girls did return home, 112 were still reported missing as of spring 2019.[1] Those who managed to escape told horrifying stories of being raped, forced into marriages, and sold into slavery. Some were even killed. The very thought of this happening to my own daughter is beyond my comprehension! I can't imagine what it would feel like to be the mother of one of those girls. To know that she was being sexually exploited, married off, sold, or possibly killed would devastate me. I imagine this is how Hadassah's cousin Mordecai must have felt when she was brought before Hegai at the start of the contest.

The young girls mentioned in Esther 2 were taken away from their families, their friends, and everything they had ever known. If they had a young man working hard to secure a dowry for their hand in marriage, it was over. If they had siblings they loved, they likely would never see them again, not to mention their parents or anyone else from their community. Their lives as they had known them were over; they lived now only to please the king. In other words, they lived to have sex with the king and possibly bear some of his children while living out their days among all the other concubines in the king's court.

In commenting about this, many prominent male Bible teachers have suggested that Hadassah, who became known by her Persian name of Esther when she was forced into the contest, used her feminine wiles to secure herself a spot as queen. This erroneous teaching implies that she was some sort of schemer at best, or a cunning seductress at worst. It is important to remember that Esther did not have a choice about entering that contest. She did not stand before King Xerxes because she hoped to seduce him for her own political gain. She didn't look at an advertisement for the beauty pageant and decide to enter it to win a scholarship or prize money. She entered because she *had* to. All the young women in the king's empire deemed lovely enough were brought before his scrutiny. Hadassah-turned-Esther was one of them.

When Esther was leaving for the palace, the final thing Mordecai told her was not to tell anyone that she was Jewish. Those were his parting instructions. Now, I don't know about you, but when my kids leave the house, my parting instructions are always the ones that I think will keep them safe—or at least give them the highest likelihood of safety! *Wear your seat belt. Pull over if you get tired.* As a mother of black children, I have an additional list of things I tell my kids in the hopes that they will stay safe. If you are black or a person of color in the United States, you know what I'm talking about! *Keep your hands where folks can see them. Be mindful how you look to others. Speak English. Don't wear a hoodie or walk that way when you're in public. If you get stopped by the police while driving, keep your hands on the steering wheel, don't ask questions, and definitely don't talk back!*

This is what social psychologists call "racial socialization." It's when children of color are given messages about being safe and having a sense of dignity and pride that white children simply don't have to consider. For example, a child from the dominant culture is able to run around in a store and touch things without the fear of being accused of stealing, while many parents of color caution their children not to pick things up or even to put their hands in their pockets when they're in a store. They're told to admire things only by looking at them and to keep their hands visible at all times while they're shopping. In an attempt to explain the necessity of these seemingly harsh instructions, parents of color must help their children understand that their success in society may not be measured by the same standards that are used to measure other children around them. I can remember my mother regularly telling me and my siblings as children, "You can't be *as good as*; you have to be *better than.*" It was like a mantra that she felt the need to drill into us. In other words, if you want to be successful in life, you have to strive to be better than the white children around you. You've got to work harder and try harder to prove yourself. You cannot just be good at something, because you will never be seen as the better candidate for the job or the better person for the scholarship. And if you want to stay safe in this world, you need to know that you may not be judged fairly and that others can get away with what you cannot.

This is what Mordecai is doing when he tells Hadassah to keep her real identity a secret. *Don't tell anyone you're a Jew.* He wants to keep her safe! That's what parents do. He wants her to survive. Even though he knows she is pretty enough to win the beauty contest, he also knows that the odds could be stacked against her because of her ethnic identity. Mordecai's advice reminds me of Martin Luther King Jr.'s dream that his children might "not be judged by the color of their skin, but by the content of their character." So, given Mordecai's last-minute urgent advice, being Jewish is clearly something that puts Hadassah's safety in jeopardy. That is when Hadassah changes her name and becomes Esther. The root of her new name in Hebrew is *hester*, which means "hidden." Changing her name and concealing her ethnic identity is the first thing she does to try to ensure her survival.

Her cousin instructs her to assimilate. *Don't be different. Blend in. Hide who you really are.* And Esther heeds his parental instructions. From her response to her cousin we see that, in addition to being pretty, she is a young woman of great character. When I was her age, I shrugged off advice like that from my parents, but not Esther. She is teachable and humble enough to listen to her cousin, and it probably saved her life. What a wise young woman! We can learn so much from her because we know that one does not become wise and teachable overnight. No, those qualities are developed over time. It was clearly something that had been developing in our heroine over the course of her life, and it comes into full fruition in this crucial moment.

Before we move on, however, let's be clear: this is not an attempt to give general long-term advice advocating for ethnic minorities to sell out or code-switch in order to accept or affirm the status quo of the dominant culture. It is also not an attempt to suggest that people of color should do anything to stay in good standing with "the white man," including betraying their own people. Although I fully understand why ethnic-minority parents give their kids instructions to fit into the culture around them, this doesn't lessen the fact that assimilation is painful. It is a truly terrible thing to have to erase essential elements of who you are in order to fit in and survive in a new culture. Do you know what it's like to have to change your name? Your language? Your persona? Your clothes? Your food? It's harder than it might seem to change your name from Francisco to Frank or to eat a peanut-butter-and-jelly sandwich when all you've ever known is rice and kimchee. It's like losing a part of your identity, denying yourself and rejecting your culture. This shift can be subtle, and the pressure to change oneself to fit into the dominant culture often happens when children are very young.

A painful example of this showed up in my Facebook feed in a post by a dear friend and colleague of mine, who is Chinese, about his two young daughters. He wrote: "My daughters face lunchbox moments every week in a city as 'multicultural' as New York City. My eldest (2nd grade) regularly tells me that classmates (white and black) make fun of her lunches. (She's been requesting only sandwiches for the past few weeks.) My youngest (kindergarten) is just encountering this. I feel angry, defeated, and defiant by this."[2]

It's extremely important to understand and name this truth that many racial and ethnic groups experience on a daily basis in order to negotiate the social reality of the world around them. One specific form this can take is a practice often referred to as *code-switching*, which describes the ways people move back and forth between different languages and ways of communicating depending on their social context. This is an intentional and strategic decision of survival and defiance. Some sociocultural linguists suggest that when speakers seek approval in social situations, they are more likely to converge their speech with that of the other speaker. This can take various forms, including the language they choose to speak, their accent, or the slang or dialect they use in conversation. When, for example, a person of color goes in for a job interview at a dominant-culture workplace, they will instinctively choose to use standard English as opposed to using vernacular speech. Similarly, an international student will change their name to make it easier for others to pronounce.

In contrast to this type of convergence, *divergent speech* is when a speaker emphasizes the social distance between themselves and other speakers by using speech with linguistic features characteristic of and familiar only to their own cultural group. For example, speakers of more than one language may use elements of multiple languages to converse with each other more deeply, without the need to be guarded or restrained, or to protect their communication from others around them who don't understand.

There is a difference between, on the one hand, forgetting who you are or denying your identity and, on the other hand, using adaptive strategies to survive. The latter results from knowing how one is perceived by society and being aware of one's diverse identities as a person who must learn to navigate "the system." This is what the renowned African American sociologist, historian, author, and civil rights activist W. E. B. Du Bois refers to as "double-consciousness." It is a concept that Du Bois first explored in his 1903 publication *The Souls of Black Folk*, in which he describes the sensation of feeling as though your identity is divided into several parts, making it difficult or impossible to have one unified identity. Du Bois spoke of this within the context of race relations in the United States. He explained that double consciousness forces black people not only to view themselves from their own unique perspective but also to view themselves as they might be perceived by the outside white world. This, said Du Bois, results in the psychological challenge of always "looking at one's self through the eyes of others." Consequently, blacks can suffer from a damaged self-image shaped by the perceptions and treatment of white people. Black life and that of others with marginalized identities, in turn, can easily become shaped by stereotypes perpetuated by mainstream culture. Du Bois explores this strange phenomenon when he writes,

> It is a peculiar sensation, this double-consciousness, this sense of always looking at one's self through the eyes of others, of measuring one's soul by the tape of a world that looks on in amused contempt and pity. One ever feels his twoness—an American, a Negro; two souls, two thoughts, two unreconciled strivings; two warring ideals in one dark body, whose dogged strength alone keeps it from being torn asunder.
>
> The history of the American Negro is the history of this strife—this longing to attain self-conscious manhood, to merge his double self into a better and truer self. In this merging he wishes neither of the older selves to be lost. He

does not wish to Africanize America, for America has too much to teach the world and Africa. He wouldn't bleach his Negro blood in a flood of white Americanism, for he knows that Negro blood has a message for the world. He simply wishes to make it possible for a man to be both a Negro and an American without being cursed and spit upon by his fellows, without having the doors of opportunity closed roughly in his face.[3]

It is the "dogged strength" to survive the psychosocial tensions of double-consciousness that produces the resilient survival skills employed by Esther and so many other ethnic minorities after her, including me.

Yes, I know exactly how this feels and can remember feeling it acutely when I went to Fuller Theological Seminary in Pasadena, California. I applied to seminary because I wanted to prepare myself to have a deep, well-informed understanding of Scripture to support my sense of calling to preach. Although I loved the small Pentecostal church I grew up in, the literal reading of the Word of God that I was accustomed to in my congregation was not able to answer my burning questions about what the Bible actually taught, specifically about whether women were called to preach. That's why I drove across the entire country with a friend and all my earthly possessions to attend Fuller Seminary. It was a great place for me to study the Word of God and develop a clear and theologically rigorous foundation to support my calling and desire to be faithful to God. However, it was also a place where I discovered that as a Black woman in White evangelical spaces, I was once again being shaped by the dominant culture around me.

I saw this most clearly when it came time to preach my first sermon in homiletics class. While I was still deciding which text I would preach from, I took a drive to Hollywood with a group of friends who, like me, were new to the West Coast. Hollywood wasn't as glamorous as I'd expected! As we rode around looking for famous spots, I saw a young girl in a big blond wig and realized that she was a teenage prostitute. I stared at her in disbelief, and my heart broke. When I got home, I prayed for the young woman I'd seen and was reminded of the text in Scripture where Jesus heals Peter's mother-in-law of a fever. I looked it up and studied the word "beseeched" in the Greek. I learned that it meant "to plead" or "beg." So I wrote a sermon titled "Are You Pleading with Him?" and a few days later preached it in my class. It was about the social brokenness in our world and our need to plead with God to heal us. I shared about the young girl in the wig, and I preached with power, clarity, and conviction. My classmates, all of whom were male, stood to their feet, giving me a standing ovation! However, when it came time to grade my sermon, my professor gave me an A for my delivery and a C-minus for my exegesis (critical explanation or interpretation of a text, especially of Scripture). I was crushed. What more could I have done? I had no idea what else they wanted from me.

That was the beginning of me losing myself at Fuller. I became more insecure and felt that I was being perceived as an emotional Pentecostal without any intellectual depth. So I tried harder and harder to prove that I was smart. Over time, I learned how to do all the scholarly and theologically substantive research that was expected of me. But by the end of the semester, when I preached my final sermon—on Psalm

27, encouraging God's people not to fear—I was afraid! Although I got an A on that sermon because I'd done thorough exegetical work, I didn't feel the spiritual power I had felt during my first sermon. In all my efforts to assimilate and be accepted in this white evangelical institution, I had lost some of the cultural and spiritual power that defined me.

Three years later, I graduated from Fuller and was invited back to participate on a panel about women and racial equality. I arrived a little later than planned, so I didn't have much time to prepare or write down my thoughts before the discussion started. I hurried to the bathroom, grabbed a paper towel, and scribbled a few notes to remind myself of the main points I wanted to share. Then I put the paper towel inside a file folder and took my place at the table as a member of the panel. When my turn came, I opened the folder and gave a few preliminary remarks. Since I didn't have anything more written on paper, I decided to wing it and speak straight from my heart. I spoke about the woman at the well from John 4. I shared the spiritual, cultural, sociological, and theological convictions I held about that Samaritan woman. It was amazing! Afterward, several people from Fuller came up to ask for a copy of my notes and praised my hermeneutical insights. I couldn't believe it! It was in that moment that I came back to the person I was before I came to Fuller. That night, I reclaimed who I was—the Black, Pentecostal woman who is smart *and* speaks from the fire of the Holy Ghost! I was no longer trying to fit in or be accepted. That experience freed me and set me on a path of knowing who I am and where my power lies.

When individuals or groups are forced to live in two social worlds, their adaptive strategies and commitment to thrive declare their human dignity in the midst of a potentially dehumanizing situation. It affirms that we are created in the image of God and that nothing can take away our capacity to love, to experience joy, and to have the audacity to hope. Refusing to give up and choosing to live in spite of the challenging circumstances we may face is actually a brave act of resistance!

When Hadassah becomes Esther, she does more than change her name. She fully blends into her new context and culture, just as her cousin instructed her. Lest you think that was easy, consider what she has to do in order to successfully assimilate. She has to speak a different language—and not just speak it but speak it well enough to pass. She is what sociologists might call "culturally competent." She is bilingual and can clearly hold her own in this new, cross-cultural situation.

Although people of color and those from the dominant culture have very particular and distinctive work they must do in the fight for racial justice and social equity, it is vital that all of us who call the United States home recognize the unique way we have been socialized in relation to the rest of the world. For too long now, being born and raised in the United States has tended to mean acting as if people in other countries must learn about and understand *us*, as though we were the epicenter and the rest of the world revolved around us. However, we now live in an increasingly connected global society and can no longer function from this posture of assumed distant superiority. Therefore, those of us who truly want to be culturally competent, globally relevant, and socially active reconcilers must learn to speak other languages.

Most people in the United States are among a minority in the world who speak only one language. Maybe this is because for a long time we were so self-sufficient that it didn't matter what we knew about other people or the languages they spoke. There wasn't a need for us to learn to communicate with them in their mother tongue. Instead, we felt like they had to learn English because we were the center of the universe. So, clearly, they ought to have known what we knew because we perceived ourselves as being the best people on the planet. Well, that reality is shifting, and new skills are now being required of all of us.

That's one of the reasons why I'm learning to speak Spanish fluently. I spent a month in Costa Rica at language school because I truly believe that anybody who wants to participate in reconciliation needs to demonstrate cross-cultural competency, which begins by learning another language and being teachable. Although I have advanced degrees, in Costa Rica I felt like I was at the level of a third grader on a good day! Learning another language has a way of making us humble. It makes us acknowledge that we need people from every level of society to help us, educate us, and enlarge our understanding of the world. Learning another language also allows us to have interactions with people from different walks of life. As we do, we admit that we desperately need them in order to survive. It makes us relate with people who are unlike us and learn something about other people that we do not know. It also gives us empathy for how it feels to be in another country and not understand what is being said. It really gives us the experience of being an outsider, someone who needs help. And then, if we are going to keep learning the language, we must find people whom we can continue to converse with when we return to our normal life. Who knows? Maybe, as it did for Esther, learning another language will save your life!

Some see Esther as just magically being in the right place at the right time to save her people. But I think there is a lot more to it than that. This isn't just a lucky coincidence. Esther was prepared. She was ready when the opportunity arose because she had done the work ahead of time. She knows the language, understands the context of the other people in her immediate surroundings, and listens to the counsel of her cousin.

Most people think that a person either is or is not a leader. We think that if we are meant to be a reconciliation leader, it will be obvious and things will just fall into place for us. But that's not how it works. We have to put in our time. We have to study. We have to learn. We have to prepare ourselves and deepen our character and competency so that we are ready when the opportunity presents itself. And it will. The question is whether we will be ready when it does.

Many years ago I was talking with an evangelist from Venezuela about my desire to speak Spanish and minister within Latin America. Do you know what his response was? He told me that the depth of my preparation would determine the length of my longevity in Latin America. And he was right! I'm still not fluent in Spanish, but I'm really trying to do the work. I'm preparing myself. I'm studying, reading, and learning about social issues from my Latina/o friends and colleagues so that if and when the opportunity presents itself, I'll be ready.

This is what Esther did, and this is what we all must do. We have to prepare ourselves. We have to continue to cultivate our character over time and learn from others. We don't know what social or political context might collide one day with our own personal context and cause us to spring into action. But if we don't lay the groundwork, we won't be ready when it does.

FIVE

PALACE LIVING

Xerxes liked Esther more than he did any of the other young women. None of them pleased him as much as she did, and right away he fell in love with her and crowned her queen in place of Vashti. . . .

When the young women were brought together again, Esther's cousin Mordecai had become a palace official. He had told Esther never to tell anyone that she was a Jew, and she obeyed him, just as she had always done.

Esther 2:17, 19–20

EVERY YEAR Oxford Dictionaries selects a word that it deems the most important term or expression in the public domain during that specific year. The word of the year is often a vital indication of a single concept that has held the public's attention and best describes the mood and attitude of people worldwide. In 2016 the international word of the year was "post-truth." This adjective is defined as "relating to or denoting circumstances in which objective facts are less influential in shaping public opinion than appeals to emotion and personal belief." The "post" in "post-truth" does not refer to *after* so much as it signifies an atmosphere in which the very notion of truth is irrelevant to begin with. This word was selected after the dictionary's editors noted a roughly 2,000 percent increase in its usage over the year 2015. This popular political practice of stretching the truth by repeatedly asserting positions disconnected from factual data to support or verify it was appearing with far more frequency in news articles and on social media in both the United Kingdom and the United States. Oxford Dictionaries president Casper Grathwohl said in a statement, "It's not surprising that our choice reflects a year dominated by highly-charged political and social discourse. Fueled by the rise of social media as a news source and a growing distrust of facts offered up by the establishment, post-truth as a concept has been finding its linguistic footing for some time."[1] This is the type of sociopolitical climate that leads to isolation and breeds an environment of misinformation and fear. And it is into this post-truth environment that we are called to go as reconcilers. However, we will not be able to be God's agents of reconciliation if we stay secluded in worlds that keep us from the reality of what is happening around us. That's what Esther will soon discover.

Hadassah-turned-Esther now finds herself in a place of literal palace living. Her beauty, poise, gracefulness, character, and intelligence won her favor with everyone she encountered, especially the king. Immediately after he saw her, Esther was crowned the new queen and now she lives in the palace. It wasn't the life she'd planned, but it also isn't as bad as she had feared. She has attendants who wait on her hand and foot. Esther now has privilege, power, and position as one living in the palace. She is at the pinnacle of prestige, with access to the king and the ability to influence those around her. Esther was privy to the best the kingdom had to offer: food, medicine, resources—you name it. Her new social position in the kingdom afforded her special rights and privileges. What more could she possibly want? Most people probably think of Esther at this point and picture a fairy tale come true.

But there is a downside to living in the palace. Esther became isolated and insulated from what was happening outside the palace walls. She was ignorant of the real issues and problems that were negatively affecting average people's lives. She had been tucked away in the inner courts for over two years by the time she became queen, and she was well insulated there, surrounded by all the creature comforts she could ever want. Yet even as she was safe, warm, fed, and clothed, wanting for nothing, she was cut off. She didn't get to chat with her old friends and neighbors anymore. She rarely saw her cousin. She was ignorant of life for those people who lived beyond the palace gates.

The problem with living in this type of ignorance and isolation is that it serves to augment fear. Ignorance and isolation feed off our fear, and vice versa. This is why fearmongering is such a powerful political tool. It doesn't appeal to the best in us. It appeals to the base in us. We sense a threat or a potential danger, and then we use inaccurate assumptions and sound bites to assuage the fear. For instance, in spite of the anti-Muslim rhetoric prevalent today, we currently have nearly six thousand self-identified Muslims serving in our armed forces.[2] Muslims have the second-highest level of education among major religious groups in our country.[3] When there have been attacks by anti-American terrorist groups, more likely than not it was Muslims who alerted law enforcement.[4] So why do we, as a culture and a country, persist in the Islamophobic views that go against the data? I don't think it's because we are bad or terrible people. I think it's because we are afraid. We've allowed fear to so block our vision that we can't see what's going on right in front of us.

Physiologically we don't think clearly when we are afraid. If we encounter or perceive a potential threat, our blood vessels constrict and our muscles tense. Many physiological changes take place in our body when we believe we are in some kind of danger, and a primitive response takes place within us. It's the way God has wired our bodies for survival. When we need to react quickly, the brain shuts down complex thinking and reverts to a fight-or-flight response. However, God has *not* given us a spirit of fear. God has given us a spirit of power and of love (2 Tim. 1:7). So when we sense the clenching grip of fear in our chests and feel within us the self-protective pull to look out for me and mine, we must choose a different way. We have to choose *not* to nurture it.

Unfortunately, hate crimes are on the rise in the United States, stoked in part by the fear-based rhetoric of politicians. This may be why, on December 15, 2015, a man with a gun walked into a convenience store in Grand Rapids, Michigan.[5] He walked over to the counter and demanded that the clerk give him money. After he had a bag full of cash, he turned his attention to another employee, a thirty-four-year-old man from India named Tony. The robber perceived

Tony to be Muslim and forced him into a storage room, where he put the gun in Tony's mouth. He called him a terrorist and said, "I killed guys like you in Iraq, so I don't even think twice about shooting you."

Thankfully, Tony, who is not actually a Muslim, survived the shooting, but Islamophobia has been on the rise since September 11, 2001,[6] and has only grown with the open embrace of anti-immigrant and anti-Muslim rhetoric in the highest offices of the United States. In the months that followed the terrorist attacks in Paris and San Bernardino, California, in late 2015, the rate of suspected hate crimes against Muslims in the United States tripled.[7] It is quickly becoming a commonly held belief among Americans that Muslims are dangerous and anti-American.

Living in isolation and insulation allows us to develop these prejudices based on post-truth rhetoric. Author, lecturer, and former educator Nathan Rutstein describes it like this: "Prejudice [is] an emotional commitment to ignorance."[8] And it's an atmosphere of isolation that lends itself so handily to prejudice and the many untruths about people—such as anti-Muslim sentiment—that are born out of fear rather than fact. When people are ignorant of the truth, they will accept any lie, and lies left unchecked can become dangerous when acted on, as with the man in Grand Rapids.

I have experienced this reality personally, including in one particular encounter that is indelibly imprinted in my memory. I had been invited to speak at an evangelical women's conference in Kansas City, Missouri, and decided to bring my daughter, Mia, with me. She was in junior high school at the time, and I wanted her to have an opportunity to experience my ministry when I travel. My administrative assistant, Betzy, also came with me to handle logistics, and we decided that Mia could help her manage the book table. During my sermon from the book of Esther, in a part where I spoke about unlikely leaders, I mentioned that Barack Obama was a student at Occidental College when I worked there as an assistant chaplain. My intent was simply to illustrate that I never would have guessed this young freshman student would one day become the president of the United States.

The sermon went very well, and the audience applauded approvingly at the end. I was in the "glory cloud" as I left the stage! While I was walking through the auditorium on my way to my book table, I noticed a middle-aged white woman running to catch up with me. I assumed she wanted to thank me for my message. But when she caught up to me in the foyer, she came right up to my face and yelled, "Why did you say that?! Why did you say Barack Obama?!" I was dazed and didn't know how to respond. I tried to explain that he was a student for one year at Oxy, thinking that maybe she didn't understand. But in a fit of rage, she shouted, "Why didn't you say Sarah Palin?!" Dumbfounded, I replied, "She didn't go to that school!" I was caught off guard and had no idea what she was talking about. She didn't have a gun, but her words were loaded.

The exchange took place in front of a lobby filled with people standing at different ministry booths. Not one person did a thing to help me. No one asked this woman to please stop or control herself. Eventually, my fourteen-year-old daughter came from behind my book table to help me. As the woman continued to yell, she accused me of mentioning Barack Obama's name as a political ploy to condone abortion policies. My daughter said, "My momma didn't even say that!" I quickly put her behind my back, trying to protect her from this woman. Finally, Betzy came into the lobby and saw what was happening. She stood between me and the woman and said as authoritatively as I've ever heard her speak, "That's enough! We're done!" Then the woman began to walk away, still yelling and accusing Barack Obama and me of being baby killers. As she left, she ended her tirade by saying, "I forgive you."

I'm not sure I'll ever forget that experience. It was frightening. Afterward, I talked to the president of the organization about the incident. She apologized profusely and made a public statement from the stage saying how inappropriate it was. Later, I learned that the woman who angrily confronted me was a board member of that ministry! Knowing that confirmed what I already knew—Christians are not isolated from the polarized political divisiveness that has become commonplace in the United States and around the world. That's why I have since added a security clause to my speaking contracts: there is a real danger for those of us who stand as reconcilers in the palaces of white evangelical spaces.

The current sociopolitical climate, where untruths are allowed to go unchecked, unchallenged, and unsubstantiated, creates an environment that not only threatens people's physical safety but also does violence to their sense of identity. Without a narrative that affirms all people as made in the image of God, some individuals in society will learn to live with and submit to the narrative of the oppressor or the oppressed that undermines their ability to reach their God-given potential. In his book *Reconciliation*, Catholic priest and theologian Robert Schreiter writes, "Violence tries to destroy the narratives that sustain people's identities and substitute narratives of its own. These might be called 'narratives of the lie,' precisely because they are intended to negate the truth of a people's own narratives."[9] He goes on to say, "It is only when we discover and embrace a redeeming narrative that we can be liberated from the lie's seductive and cunning power."[10] This is our work as reconcilers. We must awaken this reality in society by offering a larger narrative to which people can connect and rebuild their story. However, we can't do that if we stay locked inside our own little humanly manufactured palaces.

Esther had to come face-to-face with her position, her privilege, and her power after she became queen. As with so many of us, when her levels of position, privilege, and power increased, so too did the unintended distancing from other people. The longer we are in the palace, the easier it becomes to stay in the palace. Like Esther, we have to be intentional if we are going to come out of the palace. We have to work at it. It is not just going to happen on its own. Esther doesn't know anything about what's happening to people outside the palace gates. I call this the Esther syndrome, and we see it playing out everywhere. Whether we were born standing on one of the top rungs of the ladder or we've managed to scrape and pull ourselves up, inch by incremental inch, we don't want to look down. We often don't want to know about who is beneath us. We'd rather cling fast to our own position than consider reaching down to help someone further down or, heaven forbid, giving up our spot altogether!

If we're not intentional, we can all be in danger of becoming palace people. It's easy to isolate and insulate ourselves. We do it without even trying. We listen to just one news

source. We read the same paper every day. We hang out with
the same people. We stay busy all day, every day. We schedule
our children and ourselves until we're exhausted and blue in
the face. We take the freeway so that we can go around the
neighborhoods we would rather not enter. We drive rather
than walk. We choose entertainment that makes us feel
comfortable. Our social media becomes an echo chamber
of our own beliefs, opinions, and fears. We eat food that is
familiar and walk on streets that others have deemed safe.
We surround ourselves with people and things and comforts
that further enforce who we already are and how we already
think. It's truly the easiest way to live. But is it the *best* way?

Insulating ourselves and living in isolation leads to ignorance. We don't know what we don't know! Isolation and
insulation are what make it possible for someone to go about
their day, living on their cul-de-sac, not realizing that there
is someone sleeping on the street just two blocks down. It
is what makes it possible for Americans to throw away 40
percent of our food while others in the world are starving to
death.[11] Isolation and insulation are what enable us to buy
a new pair of shoes or pick up some Christmas decorations
without realizing that it was likely slave labor that brought
them into existence.[12]

In order to counteract this cycle of isolation, insulation,
and ignorance, we need to examine three things: our position, our privilege, and our power. Now, some of you might
look at those three things and think, *Nope, doesn't apply
to me because I'm broke.* Or, *I don't have any power.* Or,
I'm not white so I don't have any of those things. But let's
reconsider. It's true that you might not have what you consider position, privilege, or power, but you participate in

palace living if you're an American just by residing in the United States. You really do! Think about it: We don't have a caste system. We don't have the dire conditions that exist in so many other places in the world. We have access to social services and health care and so many other resources and opportunities. We have agency. We can vote. We can protest in the streets when we witness injustice. It's not perfect, but even the person on the lowest rung of the ladder has position, privilege, and power that needs to be grappled with, even if it looks different than it does for the person up on the very top rung.

Now, that said, it's also true that everyone is *not* culpable in the same ways. Those at the top of the hierarchy will inevitably have more work to do than those at the bottom. We don't like to hear this in America, because we want to believe that everyone is equal—but it's simply not true. The problem with this thinking is that it lacks an understanding of the specific work required for different racial groups based on historical and social realties. Not everyone will need to give up the exact same things, and not everyone is privileged in the same ways.

We must use what Jennifer Harvey refers to as a "particularistic ethic," which responds in culturally specific ways to our distinct relationship to privilege and power and the injustices that can result.[13] That means we must all examine and acknowledge our position, privilege, and power while also recognizing that some of us have much less systemic influence and authority than others and, consequently, much less to give up.

It is into our various spheres of influence that people like Mordecai come to help us recognize the issues happening outside the palace. We need to listen to these prophetic

voices—protestors, teachers, journalists, artists, preachers—
that come to get our attention and inform us about the reality
of what's going on in people's lives. This is how we break
free from the palace mentality to fight against prejudice and
injustice. If we want to understand reality and move beyond
the rhetoric of fear, we have to be intentional. We have to
examine our lives from multiple angles: How am I isolating
myself? How am I insulating myself? In what ways is this
making me ignorant? What is my position—in my family, my
church, my job, my neighborhood, and in the larger world?
What are my privileges? In what ways am I advantaged over
the people lower down on the ladder, regardless of how I got
here? And what sort of power do I have?

Esther was thrust into one of the highest positions of
power. You might not be the queen of Persia, but you do
have some type of power—some ability to effect change. As
we recognize this, it's important for us to come out of the
palace and use our access, influence, relational networks,
and power to combat the lies that inhibit the flourishing of
all God's people.

SIX

THE PROPHETIC POWER
OF LAMENT

When Mordecai heard about the letter, he tore his clothes in sorrow and put on sackcloth. Then he covered his head with ashes and went through the city, crying and weeping. But he could go only as far as the palace gate, because no one wearing sackcloth was allowed inside the palace. . . .

When Esther's servant girls and her other servants told her what Mordecai was doing, she became very upset and sent Mordecai some clothes to wear in place of the sackcloth. But he refused to take them.

Esther 4:1-2, 4

THERE IS an insidious and growing evil at work among us that continues to commodify and dehumanize human beings according to a racial hierarchy. This is rooted in a philosophical belief that certain people are higher on the "great chain of being" than others, which justifies mistreating people deemed "lower" as less than human. That's why a white man can have a gun in his hands and be arrested without being shot or killed, but a Black child holding a toy gun is killed by the police within two seconds of their arrival, before he even has a chance to speak. This type of racialized injustice is woven throughout every aspect of our human society, and I feel compelled to come "out of the palace" and speak out against it. If I and others do not call people to tell the truth about what's happening, we will replicate this type of racial evil from one generation to the next. If we refuse to face the truth about our racialized society, we will find new ways to repackage it and will never heal the pervasive racial and social injustice in our land.

That's why I must tell the truth about what happened to Eric Garner, a forty-three-year-old husband and father of six living on Staten Island.

On July 17, 2014, Eric, who was once a horticulturist for the New York City Department of Parks and Recreation and who was known by his friends and family as a generous and kind peacemaker, was approached by a few police officers on Bay Street. He was just hanging out, selling "loosies"—individual cigarettes—for some extra cash, when the police stopped and questioned him. This had happened before, but this time he is reported as having said, "I was just minding my own business. Every time you see me, you want to mess with me. I'm tired of it. It stops today."[1] I can absolutely imagine his frustration. What's the big deal? Why did they need to constantly harangue him about something so minor?

Some of the officers touched Garner, and he swatted their hands away, saying, "Don't touch me, please." One of the officers, in an attempt to subdue him, put him in a choke-hold from behind—a practice that was explicitly banned by the NYPD in 1993. On a cellphone video, Garner can be heard repeatedly saying, "I can't breathe." He wasn't resisting. Some other officers then joined in wrestling him to the ground, and one of them pushed Garner's head into the sidewalk. Garner said again, "I can't breathe," but the officers left him there and did not offer him any assistance. He lay there for a full seven minutes before anyone thought to offer any help. He died there on the sidewalk, and all of it was caught on video. The medical examiners ruled his death a homicide by neck and chest compression. He had been choked to death for selling loose cigarettes and standing up for himself when the police insisted on harassing him.

When the news of the nonindictment of the police officers responsible for strangling and killing Eric Garner reached me, I was still in Ferguson, Missouri, meeting and organizing and planning. On our last day, one of the men in our group looked down at his phone and saw the news of the nonindictment, and something unexpected happened.

He broke down. He broke down right there. He was so distraught that he had to be taken out of the room. He made it to the hallway, where he continued to shake and cry and rock back and forth. He was in agony. The rest of us surrounded him, somewhat awkwardly, and someone suggested that we sing a song of lament. We were all eager to support this man and be in the moment with him, and someone in the group led out with "Enemy's Camp," a Christian chorus that is well-known in some Black churches. While this is a powerful song about reclaiming what Satan has stolen from

God's people, it struck me and a few other folks in our group as ill-fitting for the situation. It wasn't the right song. We needed a song of despair, of grief, and of sadness. We truly needed a song of lament!

Even though most of us in the room had been reared in the African American church, which has a rich historical tradition of lamenting the social evils of our world, we no longer seemed to know how to do it. We'd lost our ability to lament—to sit in sadness and grief and despair. Standing in the hallway that day, part of a well-intentioned group that was, to be honest, fumbling along in our attempt at solidarity, I realized that we need to regain our ability to lament—collectively *and* as individuals. It is something we are called to as followers of Christ, and a perfect example can be found in the book of Esther.

Life was going well for Esther in the palace until the day she learned that her cousin Mordecai was dressed in sackcloth and ashes, looking like a mess, outside the palace gates. He was making a public spectacle of himself, weeping and wailing in front of the palace. Esther couldn't believe it! She had no idea what was going on that would cause her cousin to behave in such an extreme and uncharacteristic manner. She didn't know that in every province there was profound grief among the Jews with fasting, weeping, and wailing. Some put on sackcloth and ashes. Mordecai is one of them. Grieved beyond measure, he tears his clothing, dons the sackcloth and ashes, and takes to wailing outside the palace gates. Esther, however, hasn't a clue about the fate that awaits her people. She hears that Mordecai is outside the palace and in dismay, so she has her attendants send him some clean clothes.

Esther's action likely stems from two equally weighted concerns. First, she cares about Mordecai. He raised her as his own when she had nobody. He's her family, her people. She wants to take care of him, and it likely pains her to see him in this condition. However, Esther is also likely confused and unsettled by Mordecai. By sending the clothes, she is also sending him a message: *Pull yourself together! This is not like you!* She hopes the clothes will stanch her discomfort.

But do you know what Mordecai does with the clothes? He sends them back! He sends the clothes right back to Esther and continues with his very public lament. Mordecai refuses to be consoled. This is what lament looks like. It's sackcloth and ashes. It's weeping and wailing and crying out for justice. By sending back the clothes, he is making a prophetic and political statement. He is saying, *I will not let you silence me. I will not let you placate me. I will not go away quietly. I refuse to be pacified. I will not allow you to shut me up or force me to compose myself because I make you feel uncomfortable. No!*

There are some things that are worth crying about. Certain things ought to upset us and make us weep. When we hear about children being abused, lives being destroyed, or people being slaughtered in the streets, we ought to cry. We are not supposed to be indifferent to the suffering of others. That's why Bethany Barnes, a young white woman and dear friend of my son, wrote an open letter to the Emanuel African Methodist Episcopal Church in Charleston, South Carolina. It was a letter of lament and solidarity. She felt compelled to write it after she learned about the horrific murders of nine people at their midweek prayer and Bible study service. Her heart broke at the news of a self-proclaimed white supremacist shooting and killing those innocent Christian people, including the pastor, after they welcomed him into their church. After learning about this tragic event, Bethany refused to watch and do nothing! She decided to act and use her words to publicly lament and declare her solidarity with her African American sisters and brothers in Christ. This is what she wrote:

Dear Black Community,

We hear you. We validate you and your experiences even though we will never know what it's like to be discriminated against based on the color of our skin. We WILL listen to your stories, we will hear your frustrations, we will pursue any injustice we see or that you tell us about, and we will not diminish your experience. We will mourn together and we want to facilitate change.

We hear you. And we are so sorry. We have failed you; in our schools, lives, communities, government, AND churches. But we promise to do better. Starting today, right now. Your lives DO matter.

To the 5 year old precious child who "played dead" to avoid her own death, your life matters. We will not let your story be devalued, diminished, or untold. We will not let you go one day of your young life without feeling immeasurable love. We are so sorry that your life was compromised by such inconceivable hate.

To Cynthia Hurd, Susie Jackson, Ethel Lance, Rev. DePayne Middleton-Doctor, Rev. Senator Clementa Pinckney, Tywanza Sanders, Rev. Daniel Simmons Sr.,

Rev. Sharonda Singleton, and Myra Thompson, the 9 lives lost due to senseless, calculated, abundant hate . . . your lives mattered and they still do matter. We are so sorry that in your last minutes on this earth, you were told otherwise but we promise to show your families now that your lives DO matter to us.

To the woman whose life was purposefully spared, and was unfairly chosen to carry the burden of seeing a true act of evil carried out, and told to tell the true reasons why . . . your life matters. We will listen to and believe your story without breaking your character down and diminishing your experience. We will pray with you and be there for you.

To the family members and friends of those lost . . . we promise to not stand idly by and do or say nothing. We promise to speak up and stand up with and for you and all people of color in the future. We will listen. We will be your allies and not your enemies.

We will work to break the narrative and villainization of black males in America. Black men, your lives matter. We will stop the categorization and stigmatizing of black women in America. Black women, your lives matter.

We will not mock, downplay, or blatantly ignore anything that we do not understand, to make ourselves feel more comfortable and less like "the bad guys" in situations of race or inequality.

We acknowledge that hundreds of chapters of KKK groups, as well as countless neo-Nazi, white supremacy, and other racially motivated hate groups, STILL exist TODAY in AMERICA. We will no longer act like things *don't exist just because they don't affect us or our lives or make us feel uncomfortable thinking about.*

We know that colorism, classism, systematic racism, other "isms" and forms of discrimination and racial hatred exist, and that you are treated unfairly because of it.

We accept, acknowledge, and proclaim that this act of terror in Charleston, South Carolina was completely hate and racially driven. This crime would not have happened had the victims been white. We know that racism is not a thing of the past, but a thing of the present and our future if we do not do something. We acknowledge our privilege, take responsibility for our action and inaction, and want to put an end to this centuries-long narrative that is still alive today.[2]

Bethany could not just sit idly by. Her heart was broken by the events of the day. Her soul was deeply grieved by the actions and inactions of Christians in the past. Her public lament and rending of her garments was an appropriate response to the horrific hate crime that occurred in Charleston. Like the young man in Ferguson who wept, she was overwhelmed by what had occurred. Lament is a powerful concept that makes space for mourning. In a spiritual sense, lament allows individuals and communities to cry out to God in pain, to rest in hope, and to proclaim a trust that God will act. Psychologically, lament allows a cathartic release for those who are suffering and oppressed, a chance to let go of their shame and pain. Socially, lament functions as a public acknowledgment of injustice and a space for the oppressor to release their guilt through public confession that leads to healing and transformation.

In their book *Reconciling All Things*, Emmanuel Katongole and Chris Rice explain that "the first strategy of the Church in a deeply broken world is not strategy, but prayer. Lament is an action and not a response to make us 'feel better.'"[3] According to Katongole and Rice, lament challenges our proclivity for speed, distance, and innocence, which is so prevalent in the world today. They write, "The journey of reconciliation is grounded in a call to see and encounter the rupture of this world so truthfully that we are literally slowed down. We are called to a space where any explanation or action is too easy, too fast, too shallow—a space where the right response can only be a desperate cry directed to God. We are called to learn the anguished cry of *lament*."[4]

Lament is a voice that refuses to be consoled and calls us into a journey that will change and transform us at deeply fundamental levels. It is a protest against the brokenness of the world. It causes us to come face-to-face with hurting people and places that desperately need the healing presence of God. Lament forces us to come close enough to see the horror of what is really going on around us. It also allows us to tell the truth and to name the crisis for what it really is.

Lament is not despair or a cry into the void. Rather, "it is the prayer of those who are deeply disturbed by the way things are."[5] It is a way to call public attention to an egregious problem—that's why Mordecai said, *No, I will not be silent!* The same, no doubt, is true of the mother of Michael Brown, whose untimely and unlawful death brought me and the others to Ferguson. His body had been left in the street, uncovered, for over four hours while law enforcement tried to figure out what to do with him. His mother, Lezley Mc-Spadden, was, of course, devastated beyond belief. But like Mordecai, she didn't just go inside, pull down the blinds, and give up. No, she showed the world what grief looked like. She showed us what she was feeling. She stood up, time and again, in public, and spoke about her grief, her lament, her rage over the injustice of her son's death. And she continues to speak to this day. She's an activist, an author, and a truth teller. Like Mordecai, she refuses to back down. She refuses to be silenced or placated. And I imagine she will continue with her lament and her pursuit of justice for as long as she lives.

In solidarity with all those who mourn injustice, I pray that we will all become brave enough to send the clothes back! May we send the clothes back and, like Mordecai, refuse to be silenced. This might mean refusing financial support, a job opportunity, access to a social circle, or tuition assistance if such benefits come from the wrong place or if they are given in exchange for acquiescence to injustice. To embolden us on this journey, I leave us with a confession of lament. May it help us find the fortitude to face seemingly insurmountable obstacles and confront unjust systems, even when we feel tempted to be appeased. This reflection, written by a Catholic bishop named Ken Untener in 1979, is often called the Romero Prayer because it captures the life and spirit of Oscar Romero so well. Romero was the fourth archbishop of the Catholic Church in San Salvador, El Salvador. He spoke out against poverty, social injustice, assassinations, and torture. In 1980, Archbishop Romero was assassinated while celebrating Mass in the chapel of the Hospital of Divine Providence. I offer this meditation for all of us who are in the struggle and find ourselves appropriately located in the quest for reconciliation and healing around the world.

> It helps, now and then, to step back and take a long view.
> The kingdom is not only beyond our efforts, it is even beyond our vision.
> We accomplish in our lifetime only a tiny fraction of the magnificent enterprise that is God's work. Nothing we do is complete, which is a way of saying that the Kingdom always lies beyond us.
> No statement says all that could be said.
> No prayer fully expresses our faith.
> No confession brings perfection.
> No pastoral visit brings wholeness.
> No program accomplishes the Church's mission.
> No set of goals and objectives includes everything.
> This is what we are about.
> We plant the seeds that one day will grow.
> We water seeds already planted, knowing that they hold future promise.
> We lay foundations that will need further development.
> We provide yeast that produces far beyond our capabilities.
> We cannot do everything, and there is a sense of liberation in realizing that.
> This enables us to do something, and to do it very well.
> It may be incomplete, but it is a beginning, a step along the way, an opportunity for the Lord's grace to enter and do the rest.

We may never see the end results, but that is the
difference between the master builder and the
worker.
We are workers, not master builders; ministers, not
messiahs.
We are prophets of a future not our own.[6]

SEVEN

WHAT'S GOING ON?

Esther had a servant named Hathach, who had been given to her by the king. So she called him in and said, "Find out what's wrong with Mordecai and why he's acting this way."

Hathach went to Mordecai in the city square in front of the palace gate, and Mordecai told him everything that had happened. He also told him how much money Haman had promised to add to the king's treasury, if all the Jews were killed.

Esther 4:5-7

THE STORY a person tells about other people really matters. I've learned to be much more careful and conscious of the stories being told to me about others. I pay attention to who is telling the story and their purpose in telling it. I also know that where someone begins the story shapes the overall narrative being told. This was one of the primary lessons I learned when I went to Haiti to co-lead a leadership retreat for young Christian scholars with an organization called Haiti Partners. This ministry works with the Haitian church to develop leaders who will mobilize churches in deepening their faith and engaging in justice. Going to Haiti was a great experience for me. I can still remember those promising students and the warm generosity I experienced while I was there. However, that's not how my story in Haiti began.

When I first arrived, I was looking out the car window and saw a naked little boy playing in dirty water and squalor. I lifted my cell phone to take a picture and heard the Holy Spirit say to me, "What story will you tell?" Instantly, I felt a sense of conviction, so I closed the camera and put my cellphone down. As I sat there silently pondering what God was saying to me, I realized that the story of impoverished children has been told countless times all over the world. People from other countries, nonprofit organizations, and mission agencies have exploited the story of Haiti's poverty to raise money by showing pictures of poor black and brown children. In that moment, I knew that story had already been told too much. As I sat thinking and again looking out the window, I felt God asking me to open my eyes and my heart to see and tell another story. And that's exactly what I decided to do.

I learned from the books that I read during my visit that Haiti was founded because of the only successful slave revolt in the history of the world! After the Haitians won their freedom, the French tried repeatedly to reenslave them. In addition, no other countries—including the United States—would do business with them. Although these countries had purchased crops produced by Haiti's slave labor, they refused to help the economy of the free Haitian people. So with no international support or protection, the Haitians built a citadel to protect themselves from being reenslaved rather than investing in their infrastructure. This story is of a proud and resilient people who chose freedom over slavery, even if it meant living in poverty. I learned that the people of Haiti have been through more, withstood more, and fought back against more injustice than most people can even imagine. Those are the people I met: people of dignity and respect, of warmth and hospitality. I met people who—in their poverty—poured out great generosity on those of us visiting from the United States. That was my experience, and that is the story I will tell!

As a result of that experience, I've learned to be more careful to recognize who's telling the story and what narrative they're trying to spin. I am more leery, watchful, and suspicious because I know that often the story told is tied to some agenda or purpose that's not being overtly stated. That's why it's important to learn what's really happening and to hear the story from trusted people who are living close to and being personally affected by the situations we seek to address.

As we saw in the previous chapter, Esther was so isolated within the palace walls that she had no idea what was going on outside. She hadn't even *heard* of the decree to kill the entire Jewish population until she heard about Mordecai in sackcloth and ashes outside the palace gate. That's how Esther learned about the edict to destroy her people. Through the lament of Mordecai, she discovered what was happening outside the palace walls. Since the decree of destruction was a direct result of his own actions, Mordecai was understandably distraught when he explained what was going on.

Not long after Esther became queen, King Xerxes elevated one of his nobles, giving him the highest rank of all the nobles in his court. This nobleman, Haman, was an Agagite, a member of a minority group that had had a long, bitter struggle with the Jews. The king appointed him as prime minister, making him responsible for running the day-to-day affairs of the kingdom. We don't know why or how he got the job, but we can assume it was probably because he was effective—he got things done by any means necessary. His ruthless tactics as a demagogue no doubt caused him to garner many enemies. Maybe that's why the king himself passed a decree demanding that all people in all the provinces bow down and honor Haman on sight.

The Jews were in exile in Persia, and most exiles would still have carried the mindset of Shadrach, Meshach, and Abednego, who came before them. These young Jewish men were thrown into the furnace when they refused to bow down to Nebuchadnezzar, king of Babylon. Jews were known for refusing to pay homage to anyone but Yahweh. But in spite of this mindset, and having been worn down by their many years in exile, the Jews in the time of Esther had developed the mentality of, "When in Rome, do as the Romans do." Therefore, all the Jews probably bowed down and obeyed the Persian king's decree, along with the rest of the people—except one: Mordecai. The same man who had instructed his cousin Esther to assimilate was now refusing to compromise his own convictions. Mordecai would not bow, and that infuriated Haman!

Usually when one person offends another, their dispute is between the two of them. However, instead of settling the score with Mordecai, Haman decided to take out his anger on all the Jews. He saw his chance to destroy not just Mordecai but all the Jews throughout the king's provinces. There was historical bad blood between the Agagites and the Jews, and now Haman would take revenge for his people. To do it, Haman played on fear! Here is what he said to the king: "There is a certain people dispersed among the peoples in all the provinces of your kingdom who keep themselves separate. Their customs are different from those of all other people, and they do not obey the king's laws; it is not in the king's best interest to tolerate them. If it pleases the king, let a decree be issued to destroy them, and I will give ten thousand talents of silver to the king's administrators for the royal treasury" (Esther 3:8–9 NIV).

In essence, he's saying, "Look at *these* people! They are different. Their customs are different. They are not like us; therefore, they are less than us. They are a threat to us!" Sound familiar? This is the same type of divisive rhetoric we hear today. There are many who use stereotypes and generalizations to lump certain people from the same culture or nationality into one group. We see this played out in places like internment camps or in our efforts to determine who *might* be a terrorist. It's why one black man committing a crime means that all black men are considered suspects, or why all Mexican immigrants are accused of being "illegal aliens" who are taking away our jobs. We allow our fear to overcome us. Whenever race and ethnicity become part of the equation, we make sweeping generalizations and use those stereotypes to justify our fear and our actions. These are the roots of racial and ethnic profiling. When one individual does something unlawful or untoward, it's the profiling that dictates the response. So it is with Haman. He doesn't just deal with Mordecai but intends to destroy *all* the Jewish people in all the provinces.

Unfortunately, even the most enlightened and well-intentioned of us can be guilty of this type of stereotypical thinking based on widely held erroneous beliefs. I myself have seen this kind of "stinkin thinkin" in my own life. I was in a laundromat many, many years ago, doing laundry and minding my own business, when two young white boys came in to get a soda out of the vending machine. The machine malfunctioned. After trying unsuccessfully to get their money back, they reported it to the young Korean woman whose family owned the laundry. When she came to check out the problem, she began yelling at the boys and accusing them of lying! I remember thinking to myself, *Koreans are rude!* That was my immediate response, but then I had to check myself. I thought of all the incredible, loving, kind Korean people in my life. In fact, my daughter's godparents, Peter and Phyllis Cha, are Korean and are two of the nicest and most generous people I know. My relationship with them instantly challenged and corrected my stereotypical thinking.

Imagine what would've happened if I didn't have true Korean friends in my life. Without those personal relationships, there would've been little to pull me back from stereotyping and profiling a whole group of people after one unfortunate incident. Unlike Haman, I didn't possess the power or influence in that situation to cause real harm to others based on my stereotypes and false beliefs. But Haman was able to convince the king that he should kill all the Jews. He argued that it was not advantageous for him to tolerate or keep "those people" around. And then he sweetened the deal by offering to make it profitable for the king if he would permit them to be destroyed. In essence, Haman said, "I'll put a large sum of money into your government treasury—375 tons of silver, to be exact!"

Esther learns that couriers had sent dispatches to all the king's provinces with the order to destroy, kill, and annihilate all the Jews—young and old, women and children—on a single day, the thirteenth day of the twelfth month, the month of Adar, and to plunder their goods. A copy of the text of the edict was to be issued as law in every province and made known to the people of every nationality so they would be ready for that day.

It is important to note here that whenever people are being killed and lives are being destroyed, someone is profiting from it. For example, when US companies are allowed to export pesticides and cigarettes to other countries, even though those products are banned in the United States, someone is making money. Payday loan businesses in inner-city communities prey on the poor by allowing people to profit from charging astronomical interest rates. When it becomes a profitable business strategy to lock people away in privatized prisons, there is someone sitting at a desk in a high-rise building, probably wearing a crisp white shirt, almost certainly someone with deep political connections, benefiting from the destruction of these people's lives. This is who Haman represents—those who are behind the scenes, masterminding and profiting from the annihilation of people.

Although the bribe may have been tempting, the king was ultimately convinced on fear alone. "Keep your money and destroy the people," he essentially says. "Set a date and you've got my full support." Can you imagine? He agrees to the violent annihilation of an entire people group because he is afraid of their otherness. Tragically, this type of destruction and violence against human beings who are "other" is still taking place today. I learned about a horrible example of this while at a conference in Montgomery, Alabama. An African American minister was invited to go on a humanitarian mission to El Salvador with faith leaders from the United States. Their purpose was to learn more and to advocate for change regarding the reported violence that was occurring against the transgender community in that country.

When they arrived, they learned that 158 transgender people had been assassinated and that some had been dismembered. It wasn't clear who was doing the killing or committing these atrocities—perhaps it was law enforcement, or it may have been politically motivated or gang related. What was clear was that these crimes were not being investigated because they were not viewed as important. Some transgender leaders had to leave the country. Other LGBTQIA people were not allowed to work or they risked being fired. Still others were turned away from hospitals or supermarkets, and even churches forbade them to attend!

This minister recalled how a transgender woman standing near him had tears rolling down her face. She turned to him and said, "Every church I go to, they put me out because of who I am. Do I not have a right to know God like everybody else?" Her words broke his heart. When he returned home, he became an advocate for LGBTQIA people in the United States, people who experience the same violence and discrimination he had witnessed in El Salvador. For example, there is a legislative bill in Mississippi that follows a similar law in North Carolina that is just like those in El

Salvador. Under this legislation, an LGBTQIA person can be refused medical services, and a single mother can be refused government benefits. The law gives El Salvador the right to disregard the murders of transgender people. It's also the same kind of laws that allow us to discriminate against and harm immigrants, the poor, people with disabilities, women, people of color, and the LGBTQIA community in places all around the United States.

Once this minister became aware of the injustices against the transgender community, he was able to see and hear things he hadn't before. His heart was open. His views about the LGBTQIA community were challenged by his experience in El Salvador, and he started working to make a difference in the United States. He got proximate to pain that he had not known existed. Just as Mordecai admonished Esther to advocate for her people, this minister was moved to advocacy and action.

We may also find ourselves in a similar place. We aren't bad or unjust or unkind people. We just don't know what's going on. Or if we do know, we're not sure we can actually do anything about the political and entrenched nature of systemic evil. However, like Esther, we are now aware of the problem and we know that people's lives are being destroyed. Mordecai's lament is calling Esther and us into action. What are we going to do now? Are we willing to speak when we see injustice? I believe our answer must be yes. We must join in raising our voice in lament and advocacy for our own communities or for others who are the victims of injustice. We must refuse to sit idly by when injustice comes to call—and it comes to all of us in some form or another. Whether it's something that has caught the world's attention, like the murder of transgender people, human trafficking, or the Syrian refugee crisis, or something on a much smaller scale in our very own neighborhood, like inequity in our schools or unequal representation in our local government, we are called to speak out and advocate against injustice.

We see this calling for Christ-followers throughout the entire Bible, from the Mosaic law on through the prophets, who challenged and critiqued Israel's failures, and through the New Testament teachings of Jesus and the apostolic letters. We are called "to act justly and to love mercy and to walk humbly" with God (Mic. 6:8 NIV). We are commanded to seek justice and correct oppression (Isa. 1:17). When faced with injustice, large or small, seen by all or seen by one, may all of us, regardless of our status in society, our age, our ethnicity, or our gender identity, have the courage to cry out until justice rolls down like a river and righteousness like a never-ending stream (Amos 5:24).

EIGHT

HEALING THE DISCONNECTION

Mordecai gave Hathach a copy of the orders for the murder of the Jews and told him that these had been read in Susa. He said, "Show this to Esther and explain what it means. Ask her to go to the king and beg him to have pity on her people, the Jews!" Hathach went back to Esther and told her what Mordecai had said.

Esther 4:8-9

IN 2002, some girlfriends and I took a cruise to the Caribbean to celebrate our birthdays. On the day we went to St. Maarten, we were on the French side of the island and decided to visit an outdoor market. At one of the stands, a man was selling fresh coconuts with a straw in each one so people could drink the water inside. I watched and observed that after the person finished drinking the coconut water, the man would chop the coconut in half with a machete so they could eat the coconut meat in the middle. Intrigued, I decided to give it a try. I drank the coconut water but didn't really like it. Afterward, he cut my coconut in half, but when he opened it, the inside didn't look like what I expected! It was filled with a gooey, gel-like substance, and I was hesitant to eat it.

A Black Caribbean woman whom I'd spoken to when I walked into the market was sitting nearby eating her lunch. Observing my struggle to eat the coconut, she came over to show me how to eat it. She scooped out a little gel and gave it to me, but I was apprehensive and barely tasted it. Then she grabbed a piece of the coconut shell that was used like a spoon, scooped out some more of the gel and put it in my mouth. As she did, she said with her strong Caribbean accent, "C'mon man, be Black! You're not like those whites. Be Black!" She was basically asking me to identify with my people. She was saying, "You're one of us. Don't act like the White people who come here as tourists. Don't be like them. You're not a tourist. You're one of us. You're Black! It will hurt us if you act like White people and treat us the way they do. C'mon man, be Black!" So I ate every bit of the coconut gel as she scooped it out. In that moment, my Caribbean sister was calling me to heal the disconnection with my people through identification and proximity.

That's exactly why Mordecai had come to stand outside the palace gates. He had come to help Esther identify with and care about the plight of her people. He had to help her bridge the distance between her and the people outside the comfort and protection of her world. When Mordecai sent Esther's well-meaning gift of clothes back to his cousin in the palace, he included something else in the bundle of garments: the written decree, signed by the king, announcing the destruction and upcoming genocide of the Jews. As the writer James Baldwin once said, "If I love you, I have to make you conscious of the things that you don't see."[1] Mordecai knew that Esther was uninformed. He knew that she needed to know what was going on. He also included instructions for her to come out of hiding, go to the king, and entreat him on behalf of her people—he wanted her to speak out against this injustice!

I can only imagine that she probably said to herself, "Who, *me*? He wants me to do *what*?!" Her cousin was the one who implored her to hide her identity in the first place. He told her to keep her ethnicity a secret. "Tell no one you are a Jew," he said. Now he wants her to confess? Now he wants her to reveal her identity? After all the work she had to do to assimilate, on Mordecai's orders, now he wants to change the game plan?! Now he seems to be saying, "I was wrong. It's not all about you!"

Perhaps Mordecai originally thought that having Esther assimilate would keep her safe. He had been raising her as his own daughter, after all, so of course he wanted her to live! But when it becomes clear that other lives besides hers are hanging in the balance, he knows it's time for her to step out on behalf of her people. Assimilating may work when it's about your own comfort and well-being, but when you realize that other people's lives are at stake, you cannot be concerned only with your own personal safety or professional advancement—you have to step out.

Mordecai's call for Esther to be informed is also a call to us. Understanding current sociopolitical issues and using this information to inform our actions is crucial to being actively involved in the work of justice and reconciliation. It is vitally important that we educate ourselves about the policies and issues that negatively affect people's lives. In order to be empowered as advocates for social change and racial justice, we must be informed about what is really happening in the world around us.

Let me give you an example of what is really going on. The infographic in figure 1 shows the percentages of the general population compared to drug *prisoners* in the United States, broken down according to race. Do you see what I'm seeing? I'm seeing that the majority of the population is White. But I'm also seeing that the majority of those *imprisoned* for drug use and possession are Black and Latino. What's that about? Why the discrepancy?

Although rates of drug use and selling are comparable across racial lines, people of color are far more likely to be

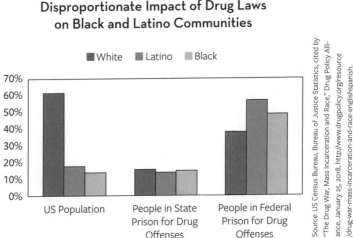

FIGURE 1

Disproportionate Impact of Drug Laws on Black and Latino Communities

Source: US Census Bureau, Bureau of Justice Statistics, cited by "The Drug War, Mass Incarceration and Race," Drug Policy Alliance, January 25, 2018, http://www.drugpolicy.org/resource/drug-war-mass-incarceration-and-race-englishspanish.

stopped, searched, arrested, prosecuted, convicted, and incarcerated for drug-law violations than are Whites. Higher arrest and incarceration rates for African Americans and Latinos are not reflective of a higher prevalence of drug use or sales in these communities but rather reflect a law enforcement focus on urban areas, on lower-income communities, and on communities of color, as well as inequitable treatment by the criminal justice system.[2]

In 1994, one of President Richard Nixon's top aides, John Ehrlichman, admitted that this law enforcement policy was intentionally racist from the very start. Here is what Ehrlichman confessed:

> "You want to know what this was really all about?" he asked with the bluntness of a man who, after public disgrace and a stretch in federal prison, had little left to protect. "The Nixon campaign in 1968, and the Nixon White House after that, had two enemies: the antiwar left and black people. You understand what I'm saying? We knew we couldn't make it illegal to be either against the war or [against] black people, but by getting the public to associate the hippies with marijuana and blacks with heroin, and then criminalizing both heavily, we could disrupt those communities. We could arrest their leaders, raid their homes, break up their meetings, and vilify them night after night on the evening news. Did we know we were lying about the drugs? Of course we did."[3]

Wow! That's similar to what happened to Anthony Ray Hinton, an African American man who spent thirty years of his life in prison on death row for a crime he did not commit. In 1985, he was mowing the lawn at the home he shared with his mother in Montgomery, Alabama. Two White detectives pulled up in a police car and asked his name. When he answered, they arrested him, handcuffing his hands behind his back. They shoved him into the back of the police car while he anxiously asked what he was supposed to have done. One of the detectives said, "Robbery and capital murder." "What's capital murder?!" Hinton asked. "You're gonna get the death penalty," the detective replied. "But I didn't do it!" Hinton said desperately. The officer turned to him and said that it didn't matter because there were five reasons why he would be convicted anyway. He said, "(1) You're Black, (2) the victim is White, (3) the prosecuting attorney will be White, (4) the judge is White, and (5) the jury will most likely be all White." Then the officer said, "Do you know what that spells? It spells conviction."[4]

The trial lasted only a day and a half. Hinton was found guilty and convicted. He spent thirty years on death row in solitary confinement. Fourteen years into his sentence, Bryan Stevenson, a civil rights lawyer and the founder and executive director of the Equal Justice Initiative, took up his case. Stevenson and his team fought for sixteen years—going all the way to the US Supreme Court. In April 2015, Hinton was finally exonerated and set free from prison! He was the 152nd of 156 people who have been proven innocent and released from death row since 1983.

Sadly, we still see this form of profiling during police stops, just as we see racial disparities in drug enforcement, achievement gaps in our school systems, and environmental policies that run along racial boundary lines taking place today. Nixon and Ehrlichman might have been prejudiced in the late 1960s, but it was their *power* that enabled them to destroy entire communities of people with their unjust laws and policies. This combination of prejudice plus power makes a person or group truly dangerous on a large, community-sized scale. It is this kind of evil that we must resist.

According to a basic dictionary definition, racism is simply the poor treatment of or violence against people because of their race, or the belief that some races of people are better than others. But I believe that while that holds true, racism is more than that. Racism is a systemic evil that robs people of their ability to thrive. It is the combination of prejudice and power that is not just a personal problem for individual people. It's a social system that affects every part of our culture and society. It's when people in power use their influence to create systemic realities that privilege their own racial group or tribe. As Rev. Dr. Bernice King, the youngest daughter of Rev. Dr. Martin Luther King Jr., rightly observed on social media, "Racism is not dislike, bias or ill will toward another race. It is the assertion of power to obstruct justice, progress and equality."[5]

In order to fight against the commingling of power and prejudice that we see in our world, our communities, and our legislature, first we need to acknowledge our past. We need to understand where we've come from in order to understand where we're heading. We cannot move forward without looking back. Bryan Stevenson explains it like this:

> We have in this country this dynamic where we really don't like to talk about our problems. We don't like to talk about our history. And because of that, we really haven't understood what it's meant to do the things we've done historically. We're constantly running into each other. We're constantly

creating tensions and conflicts. We have a hard time talking about race, and I believe it's because we are unwilling to commit ourselves to a process of truth and reconciliation. In South Africa, people understood that we couldn't overcome apartheid without a commitment to truth and reconciliation. In Rwanda, even after the genocide, there was this commitment, but in this country, we haven't done that.[6]

In 1992 in Germany, the Stolperstein Art Project was initiated by German artist Gunter Demnig. A stolperstein, which literally means "stumbling stone," is a cobblestone-size concrete cube bearing a brass plate inscribed with the name and life dates of individual victims of German Nazism. The Stolperstein Art Project commemorates "individuals at exactly the last place of residency—or, sometimes, work—which was freely chosen by the person before he or she fell victim to Nazi terror, euthanasia, eugenics, was deported to a concentration or extermination camp, or escaped persecution by emigration or suicide." While it started in Germany to commemorate those who lost their lives in the Holocaust, as of January 2015 there are now over fifty thousand stolpersteins in Germany and surrounding European countries.[7]

That is what it looks like to acknowledge the past. Germany is horrified by what its leaders and citizens did in World War II. With the stolpersteins, the country is collectively able to say, "Look at what we've done." They have given themselves a constant physical reminder lest they forget while also bearing witness to the names of the people who were brutalized, lost, or otherwise affected by what they did. In the United States, we have done nothing similar to commemorate and acknowledge our past. We refuse to face our shame. We refuse to acknowledge what it means to have done what we did to enslave human beings. We refuse also to acknowledge our confiscation of land and mass genocide against the native tribes of this land. Not only does this deprive communities of color of their full restoration; it also deprives those who are White of the chance to tell the truth and receive the healing that comes through confession. We can't have restoration and reconciliation without first telling the truth. Yet we are unwilling to do that. We won't allow ourselves the chance to tell the truth about our past, and without that truth telling we have very little hope of achieving the reconciliation we so desperately need.

Like Esther, we must realize that we can't tell the truth about what's happening unless we get better informed. To do this, we need trusted people in our lives who confront us with the truth that we may not be aware of. Sometimes this means we need to seek out alternative news sources or read books by female authors, people of color, or international voices who will challenge us to think and see the world from a different perspective. Maybe it means attending conferences on justice where we can hear speakers on various subjects who will expose us to new information.

We also, as reconcilers, must get close enough to the real facts to be able to see and know for ourselves what is actually going on in people's lives. Stevenson calls this "practicing proximity." It may sound simple, but in truth it is deeply challenging because most of us have been warned to avoid places of pain and suffering. But Stevenson argues that the first step in fighting injustice is to get proximate to injustice. This means showing up and seeing things with our own eyes. It means staying proximate to people experiencing real pain in the communities around us. It is essential that we remain rooted in a community, precisely because our theology and methodology must be grounded in our proximity and connection to real people who are facing real problems. This proximity also includes our commitment to put our bodies on the line and our skin in the game by staying present—to march in the protest, go to the border, visit the detention center, stand in solidarity, go to the shelter, and be present at the immigration raid. This is what causes us to realize that we have no other choice but to act.

When we get close enough to view the problem, we can start to imagine solutions that help us find our way to justice. I am convinced that if we get close enough to care, it literally will change our lives. Again, Stevenson sums it up like this: "When we get close, we hear things that can't be heard from afar. We see things that can't be seen. And sometimes that makes the difference between acting justly and unjustly. . . . When you get close to injustice, you will get broken, too. But I'm here as a living witness that being broken is what makes you human."[8]

So now, as in the story of Esther, the problem has been explained to us, and we are aware of the very real danger that people face. Modern-day Mordecais are challenging us to get involved. Esther can no longer pretend to be ignorant, and neither can we. The call is clear. Like Esther, we must not ignore the call when it comes, even if the timing is inconvenient or the information difficult to hear. We must take action once we learn of injustice.

NINE

BREAKING OUR SILENCE

[Esther] answered, "Tell Mordecai there is a law about going in to see the king, and all his officials and his people know about this law. Anyone who goes in to see the king without being invited by him will be put to death. The only way that anyone can be saved is for the king to hold out the gold scepter to that person. And it's been thirty days since he has asked for me."

When Mordecai was told what Esther had said, he sent back this reply, "Don't think that you will escape being killed with the rest of the Jews, just because you live in the king's palace. If you don't speak up now, we will somehow get help, but you and your family will be killed. It could be that you were made queen for a time like this!"

Esther 4:10-14

FOR YEARS I avoided speaking about sexuality for fear that I would be criticized for being too liberal. So I stayed silent. But I have learned over the years that criticism is part of doing the work of reconciliation. That's why I will no longer keep silent about the truth that *all* people are created in the image of God and, therefore, *all* people are worthy of love, protection, equality, dignity, and respect. The opportunity for me to break my silence and stand in solidarity about this came when Judy Howard Peterson asked me to be her advocate in disciplinary hearings being held by her denomination because she had performed the wedding of a gay couple.

First, let me say that Judy is one of the finest college chaplains I've ever known. Her dedication to students, her pastoral sensitivities and insights, and her excellent preaching gifts all combine to make her an outstanding campus pastor. When she was asked to perform the wedding of a former student and ministry colleague, who is a committed Christian and also gay, she agreed. She knew that if she denied this man and his partner, both of whom were committed Christians, the right to be married by the person who had been their pastor for so many years, she'd be giving them the message that they were not made in the image of God in the same way that all her other students were. So she performed the wedding.

By asking me to accompany her into the disciplinary hearings, she was asking me to be proximate and stand in solidarity with her. I was scared because I am a part of that same church denomination. I knew that, by standing with her, I was putting myself in the position of being questioned about my own beliefs on sexuality. I had to decide whether I was going to stay silent or stand for the dignity and rights of all people. This was my Esther moment, and Judy was my Mordecai, standing outside the palace gates asking me to get involved. I wasn't sure what the outcome would be for her or for me, but I knew that I didn't want Judy to walk in there alone. So I went as her advocate into the hearings.

The tension in that room was palpable. Both Judy and I prayed hard! It was not easy to endure the questions and veiled accusations, but Judy explained her reasoning clearly and with great Christian conviction. She didn't waiver, and neither did I. Unfortunately, the decision did not go in her favor. Her ministerial credentials were suspended, and she was terminated from her position as chaplain. I'm so sad about this because I believe we've lost one of our best college pastors, and it comes at a time when students desperately need one! But I will always be grateful that I was there to stand with Judy because it challenged me to dig deeper and become braver.

That's what's happening to Esther. When she first receives the decree and her cousin's plea for her to petition for her people, she hesitates. And who could blame her? First, she argues that she has no business, no right, to approach the king. She explains, further, that only those to whom the king extends his golden scepter are allowed to enter his presence. If anyone dare approach him without being called, that person will be put to death. She could be killed for approaching the king without being summoned! Of course she's scared— she stands to lose everything. All the power, prestige, and privilege that she had become accustomed to could possibly be gone in the blink of an eye. It would give anyone pause. Not to mention that the queen who had come before her had already been banished. Esther knows that the same fate could await her, or possibly even worse if she dares to step out of line.

I would also venture to guess that Esther is confused. The king doesn't know she's Jewish, and her secrecy on the matter was Mordecai's idea in the first place. I can also imagine that Mordecai was probably just as scared as Esther was herself. He knew the risks. He knew what might happen to her, and I'm sure he was tempted to have her hold her silence so that she might live. But he knows that she must speak out because there are other people, an entire nation, whose lives are on the line. How could he encourage her to keep silent when there are so many more people's lives involved?!

The risk to speak up and stand in solidarity with the oppressed was not only Esther's; it was Mordecai's as well. He too had something very precious to lose, but he took the risk to ask Esther to be brave—to identify with her people, to use her influence and access, to take the message of the oppressed and translate it so the people in power would understand. This is challenging! Esther is being asked to be the one who connects the poor to the wealthy and to create energy between them. As my friend Roy Goble, author of the book *Junkyard Wisdom*, said to me in conversation: "The poor and oppressed often live with the affliction of despair (a lack of hope), while the rich often live with the affliction of self-indulgence (a lack of faith). The poor can learn a lot from the rich about hope; the rich can learn a lot from the poor about faith. Both, of course, can teach each other a lot about love." This is precisely what Esther, in her own way, is being asked to do—to take on the role of a translator or an ally who is able to speak into a different socioeconomic reality, culture, language, and ethnic identity to help the king see differently.

This unique and critical type of allyship is an especially important role for white Christians to understand and embrace as they work for justice and reconciliation. In her novel *Small Great Things*, Jodi Picoult—a white woman—tackles the notion of allyship in her author's notes, writing,

> Most of us think the word "racism" is synonymous with the word "prejudice." But racism is more than just discrimination based on skin color. It's also about who has institutional power. Just as racism creates disadvantages for people of color that make success harder to achieve, it also gives advantages to white people that make success easier to achieve. It's hard to see those advantages, much less own up to them. And that, I realized, was why I had to write this book. When it comes to social justice, the role of the white ally is not to be a savior or a fixer. Instead, the role of the ally is to find other white people and try to make them see that many of the benefits they've enjoyed in life are direct results of the fact that someone else did not have the same benefits.[1]

It takes courage to do this, and a new understanding of what it means to pursue racial reconciliation as a white ally. I saw this type of brave allyship embodied by the pastors of my local church, who stood in solidarity to protect my life. It happened the Sunday after a violent rally in Charlottesville, Virginia, where hundreds of white nationalists, Ku Klux Klan members, and neo-Nazis came to protest the removal of a Confederate statue. They were armed with helmets, shields, and baseball bats and were carrying Confederate flags and placards inscribed with anti-Semitic slurs. In a tragic fit of racist-induced rage, a young white man attending the rally drove his car into a crowd of people who were protesting this white supremacist gathering. One woman was killed, many others were injured—some critically—and two police officers died in a helicopter crash while trying to protect the crowd.

I was scheduled to preach and knew I would have to address this tragic event in my sermon. While sitting with other pastors during praise and worship, I noticed a young white man who came right down to a seat directly in front of the pulpit. He had close-cut hair, wore a black jacket, and had sunglasses on top of his head. He looked over his shoulder from right to left, as if he were looking for someone else. My heart beat fast, and I felt a palpable sense of fear!

I tried to compose myself, not wanting to overreact. However, when our white male youth pastor repented during prayer for the sin of white supremacy, the visitor in the front row jerked his head! I turned to the pastor next to me and asked whether he knew who the man was. He said that he didn't, then added, "I feel uncomfortable too, so I've got my eye on him." Soon after, an older white man with a gray beard came and sat down by the young man. They chatted quietly. I later learned that they didn't know each other but that the older man was also concerned and decided to sit by the young man to be a calming presence. Seeing him gave me some sense of relief, but I still felt I should alert the security team of my concerns. When I returned to my seat, I learned that the other pastors had exchanged a text message and devised a quick plan to intervene if necessary.

When I went on stage, I saw the pastors, a staff person, and a lay leader sitting in the front row in various places. They each looked directly at me with an expression in their eyes that said, "You don't have to worry. We're not gonna let anything happen to you. We've got this!" It was clear that they took my safety as a Black woman seriously. They didn't minimize or dismiss my worries by suggesting that I was making too much of the situation. Nor did they sit silently by trying to decide what to do. Thankfully, nothing happened, but I knew my team had devised a plan and would spring into action if they had to. They were willing to fight to protect me. That's what real solidarity looks like! I never felt more loved and cared for by my church. It's this type of active solidarity and allyship that leads to social change and racial justice.

This is what Mordecai is calling Esther and us to, and it is scary. The temptation in the face of this challenge is to fear for our personal safety and security. Therefore, our response is often to keep quiet and not make waves or cause trouble. But Mordecai knows that this is not an option for Esther, nor is it for us. Silence is not an option! Silence has the potential to do unbelievable damage. Silence can be violent. Silence isn't passive. Silence is active, and it carries with it the power, in the case of Esther and so many others, to fuel atrocity and unthinkable hatred. Now it is time for Esther and us to venture beyond solidarity and into activism. This is precisely why we must speak, write, create art, post on social media, preach, and teach in order to make our voices heard. We know that the times in which we live are dangerous and demand a response. People are being killed in churches, in the streets, and in public schools, and lives are being destroyed. Innocent people die every day, and that will continue if we refuse to speak out against it and say something! We are well aware that political divisiveness threatens to tear our country and our world apart. But when we let this kind of divisive rhetoric go unchecked and keep our mouths shut to avoid conflict, we are contributing to the problem. When, for example, discrimination against women is endorsed by society, in the church, or in the workplace and we remain silent, we become partners in crime and complicit with the inequity happening around us.

That's exactly what happened during the Holocaust in Nazi Germany. From 1941 to 1945, Jews were systematically murdered in a genocide, which was part of a larger event that included the persecution and murder of other peoples in Europe, such as ethnic Poles, Soviet citizens, the LGBTQIA community, people with disabilities, and Jehovah's Witnesses. However, a German Lutheran pastor named Martin Niemöller refused to stay silent. In a speech to the representatives of the Confessing Church in Frankfurt on January 6, 1946, he shared his poem "First They Came." It is about the cowardice of German intellectuals following the Nazis' rise to power and subsequent purging of their chosen targets, group after group. The poignancy and power of this poem still resonate as we continue to face oppression and hatred.

> First they came for the Jews
> and I did not speak out
> because I was not a Jew.
> Then they came for the Communists
> and I did not speak out
> because I was not a Communist.
> Then they came for the trade unionists
> and I did not speak out
> because I was not a trade unionist.

Then they came for me
and there was no one left
to speak out for me.[2]

For this reason, Mordecai says to Esther, "Don't think that you will escape being killed with the rest of the Jews, just because you live in the king's palace." He's telling her that her plight is tied to their plight. What affects one affects everyone. It's as true today as it was then. You may be middle class, college educated, white, American, of the dominant culture, wealthy, or you name it, but this doesn't mean that what affects other people won't eventually affect you too! So, Esther, don't go fight *for* them. Go fight *with* them, knowing that your destiny is tied to their destiny. Your well-being is tied to their well-being. Your flourishing is tied to their ability to flourish.

Similarly, every Christian is called to speak out. Every Christian is called to be an activist. This will demand particular acts of courage to challenge and confront entrenched systems, which will look different for specific racial and ethnic groups given our unique histories. But every Christian is called to step out for the least of these, as though we were stepping out and speaking out for Jesus himself. We all have power and we all have influence. Issues of injustice are all around us, and we cannot keep silent in the face of them. The question is, Will we open our eyes to see them? Will we look at the papers that Mordecai sends us? What will we do when they come for our neighbor, our classmate, or our friend?

The attacks against the "other" in our nation and world are broad and expansive; so too must our response be. Practicing intersectionality and being an ally are more important now than ever. I understand that none of us are free until we all are free. That's why I stand against all kinds of isms and other-oriented fears—racism, sexism, ableism, homophobia, classism, and so many others. But standing against these forces is a journey that requires intention and effort. I remember a moment when I was challenged to become more inclusive in my understanding and practice of diversity. One of my students at Seattle Pacific University came by my office to discuss a concern she had about my class. She explained that she was hearing-impaired and asked me to use subtitles when I included videos in my lectures. Although my goal was to make my classes more interesting, it never dawned on me that my use of videos was unintentionally alienating some of my students. That student helped me understand that diversity includes disability. Her courage to tell me the truth helped expand my horizon of what it means to stand in solidarity with others.

Engaging with these young, emerging leaders is one of my greatest joys as a university professor. Many of my students go on after graduating to embody the value of reconciliation in their personal and professional lives. They are everyday activists in their various spheres of influence, and they give me great hope for the future, even on some of my most discouraging days. That's why I couldn't agree more with Diana Chapman Walsh, former president of Wellesley College, who said, "Can there be any doubt, then, that we need our graduates—this new American generation of such great privilege and promise—to become active participants in the world, potent advocates for human rights, confident leaders willing to take risks in the pursuit of intellectual honesty, of freedom to disagree, of justice and fairness, global citizenship, and mutual responsibility? And so the question arises then: How we can support our students in becoming passionate and powerful moral leaders?"[3]

This is why so many advocates for reconciliation teach, including me. It is one way that we refuse to keep silent. My colleague, author and philosophy professor George Yancy, affirms this in his article "I Am a Dangerous Professor":

So, in my classrooms, I refuse to remain silent in the face of racism, its subtle and systemic structure. I refuse to remain silent in the face of patriarchal and sexist hegemony and the denigration of women's bodies, or about the ways in which women have internalized male assumptions of how they should look and what they should feel and desire.

I refuse to be silent about forms of militarism in which innocent civilians are murdered in the name of "democracy." I refuse to remain silent when it comes to acknowledging the existential and psychic dread and chaos experienced by those who are targets of xenophobia and homophobia.

I refuse to remain silent when it comes to transgender women and men who are beaten to death by those who refuse to create conditions of hospitality.

I refuse to remain silent in a world where children become targets of sexual violence, and where unarmed black bodies are shot dead by the state and its proxies, where those with disabilities are mocked and still rendered "monstrous," and where the earth suffers because some of us refuse to hear its suffering, where my ideas are marked as "un-American," and apparently "dangerous."

Well, if it is dangerous to teach my students to love their neighbors, to think and rethink constructively and ethically about who their neighbors are, and how they have been taught to see themselves as disconnected and neoliberal subjects, then, yes, I am dangerous, and what I teach is dangerous.[4]

I am calling you—just like Esther, Judy Howard Peterson, George Yancy, and others—to be everyday activists who care enough to break your silence. Yes, there will be a cost. There will be personal risk. Ask Dr. Larycia Hawkins, a former tenured professor at Wheaton College, who decided to wear a Muslim headscarf in a show of solidarity with Muslim believers during the 2015 Advent season. She saw a people who were oppressed in our country and wanted to do something to show her support and her alliance with her neighbors. This seemingly simple act had significant and far-reaching consequences for Dr. Hawkins, ultimately causing her to lose her job amid national media attention. That's what personal cost looks like. It might not mean physical death, but for Dr. Hawkins it certainly meant the loss of her livelihood, her job, and her standing in that academic community. She eventually found other employment and moved on with her life, but her show of solidarity was costly. As followers of Jesus Christ and people of faith, we too are called to make costly and courageous decisions if we want to work toward the building of a better world.

It is important to understand that taking a stand for justice does not always yield the results we believe are right. Sometimes we stand up to the king and still injustice prevails. We cannot be deterred or dismayed, but we must continue to get proximate to pain and understand when we are being called to stand in solidarity with those who are being persecuted. As we move forward by faith, we must be willing to face the consequences because we know that we are risking our lives for something greater. We are agents of the kingdom of God. As the great American writer and theologian Frederick Buechner tells us, "Wherever people love each other and are true to each other and take risks for each other, God is with them and for them and they are doing God's will."[5]

TEN

INTERCESSORS FOR JUSTICE

Esther sent a message to Mordecai, saying, "Bring together all the Jews in Susa and tell them to go without eating for my sake! Don't eat or drink for three days and nights. My servant girls and I will do the same. Then I will go in to see the king, even if it means I must die."

Esther 4:15–16

I WAS a guest speaker at a conference and was talking with rap and spoken-word artist Jason "Propaganda" Petty when he said to me, "You know what? All of the prophetic voices who are primarily at the forefront of the reconciliation movement today are women." I respect his perspective because I am a huge fan of his work, so I paid close attention to what he said. He and his wife, he went on to tell me, were watching and listening carefully to the voices of women because they seem to be the source of the cutting-edge, prophetic energy that is pushing the reconciliation movement forward. After reflecting on this, I agree that women, especially women of color, have a more acute understanding of the interlocking structures of oppression. Our lived experiences inform our imagination and our methodology for leading in a more communal and equitable way.

We see this reality being lived out all around the world. Women are rebuilding communities that have been devastated and destroyed by violence, war, genocide, political corruption, and economic injustice. These women harness their strength and cultivate their leadership while managing their own grief, trauma, and pain in order to connect across divides and create a new culture of peace, stability, and unity. In spite of gender inequality and lack of educational and economic resources, these women find themselves leading reconciliation efforts that reveal the warriors they truly are.

Such was the case in Liberia during its civil war in 1989–1996, which was one of the bloodiest conflicts in all of Africa. It took the lives of more than 200,000 Liberians and displaced over a million people into refugee camps. This war between the dictatorship of the Liberian president and the rebels who wanted to overthrow the government raged on for years. Both factions terrorized the people in the country through killings, rapes, dismemberment, and destruction. Children were forced to become soldiers and commit horrible atrocities, including rape and murder. This civil war entirely destroyed Liberia's once-viable infrastructure, leaving entire villages empty as people fled for their lives. Just three years later, a second civil war broke out and lasted four more years. Whatever was left from the devastation of the first war was now completely decimated. It was a dire time in Liberia. Peace talks were stalled more often than not. So many people were displaced and killed that it truly seemed like a hopeless situation. What could anyone possibly do to help a country recover from such unspeakable horror and desolation?

Enter Leymah Gbowee and Comfort M. Freeman, two Liberian Christian women who were inspired by a dream to bring Christian women together to start a peace movement. They began within the church and asked women from all churches to come together. At one meeting, a Muslim woman went up to the podium to address the church. She told the group that she was moved by what they were doing and urged them to bring Muslim women into the peace movement. They agreed, and with this extraordinary mission, the women dressed in plain white clothes and covered their heads as a way to downplay any differences related to class or religion among them. They made peace signs and staged a daily sit-in during which they would pray at the fish market that the Liberian president drove past every morning. Although the president would not acknowledge them, these women refused to give in to the hopelessness that surrounded them on all sides. For months, they organized thousands of local women from different faiths to pray and sing in the fish market. Day after day, week after week, for months, these women gathered to pray and sing. Their mission was to "pray the devil back to hell"!

This became known as the Women of Liberia Mass Action for Peace, which mobilized over three thousand women and managed to stage peaceful protests and nonviolent sit-ins, and eventually became a political force to be reckoned with. Ultimately, the women were able to achieve peace in Liberia after fourteen years of civil wars and unrest and helped bring to power Ellen Johnson Sirleaf, the first elected female head of state in Africa. These courageous women demonstrated that in times of great desperation, prayer proved to be stronger than politics. Who would have thought that a group of women in a war-torn country would have the power to do *anything*? These women demonstrate unequivocally that prayer overrides politics and can topple governments. That's what people of faith bring to the table. Prayer is our secret weapon, and it can move mountains.

Esther was seeking a mountain-moving answer to prayer when she sent word back to Mordecai. She knew that she had to fast and pray in order to have the courage to face the king and try to save her people. There are many scholars who question whether Esther is really a spiritual book because it does not explicitly mention God. It's true that God's name is not directly included in the book, but it's also true that when Esther decides she will take a stand for her people, the very first thing she chooses to do is pray. She instructs Mordecai to spread the word to all the Jews in Susa to fast and pray for three days while she and her attendants do the same. Her first impulse is to acknowledge and seek God, and she calls on her community to do likewise.

This is absolutely instructive for us. Speaking out against injustice and standing up for righteousness begins with an understanding that we cannot simply rely on our own strength or human understanding. Esther immediately knows that she can't just come up with a game plan. She can't just call a meeting of leaders and strategists and figure things out on her own. She knows that something more is needed. Esther doesn't wonder what to do next. Her spiritual formation informs her actions. She knows she needs to seek the face of the holy and righteous sovereign God. And that's exactly what she sets out to do!

Esther knows that she must hear from God before she attempts to confront political powers and advocate on behalf of others. She models for us an activism rooted in prayer. She shows us how to speak truth to power and how to confront the powers that be on behalf of other people out of our concern for their well-being and desire for them to thrive. Theologian and author Walter Brueggemann agrees with this spiritual posture and challenges us to recognize it:

> The exclusive claim of God is linked to the *value of the brother and the sister*. God's claim is the critical principle which permits my turning away from my own good and my own interest to that of the neighbor. . . . The battle is to keep these together. In the church tradition I know best, we would prefer to rush past the matter of *God's holiness* to the question of *human justice*. In other contexts, the contrary danger may be evident. Without the holiness of God, the justice of neighbor becomes a crusade. So we must hold these together.[1]

When we pray, we affirm that justice and *shalom* begin with God and not with us. Prayer helps us reaffirm that the justice we seek starts with God's heart for justice and not our own. We might want to fix things faster and quicker, but prayer reminds us that we must trust God for everything and in all things as we move forward. Our pursuit of reconciliation is going to require faith and obedience. We need obedience because things may often unfold differently than we expect, and the direction we receive in answer to our prayers may seem odd. Prayer helps us when we cannot act in our own strength or on the basis of our own intellectual knowledge. As the prophet Isaiah reminds us, "The LORD says: 'My thoughts and my ways are not like yours'" (Isa. 55:8). We must follow God's strategy and timing because "we are not fighting against humans. We are fighting against forces and authorities and against rulers of darkness and powers in the spiritual world" (Eph. 6:12). Ultimately, the issues we are fighting against are spiritual—they are *evil*—and we cannot fight evil in our own strength. We need prayer.

Dr. Martin Luther King Jr. came to this conclusion at a very difficult time in his life and ministry. It was 1955. Late one night Dr. King was dozing off in his bedroom when the telephone rang. He answered. "Listen, n——, we've taken all we want from you. Leave Montgomery immediately if you have no wish to die," the caller hissed. King hung up and went to the kitchen to heat a pot of coffee. He had been receiving death threats for weeks—ever since he had accepted a request to lead a bus boycott in Montgomery, Alabama—and he was starting to really doubt his decision. He was afraid for his wife and their baby girl. He was trying to figure out how to relinquish his role as the boycott leader without looking like a coward.

Then something happened that King would talk about for years afterward. He bowed over his untouched cup of coffee and prayed aloud in desperation. As he sat there, his head in his hands, King said he heard an "inner voice" that addressed him by name and encouraged him to stand up for justice. The experience reminded Dr. King that he could not depend on the resources of his own talents and intellectual training to make it in the struggle. He had to depend on God.

Here's what he said about the experience:

> The words I spoke to God that midnight are still vivid in my memory. "I am here taking a stand for what I believe is right. But now I am afraid. The people are looking to me for leadership, and if I stand before them without strength and courage, they too will falter. I am at the end of my powers. I have nothing left. I've come to the point where I can't face it alone."
>
> At that moment, I experienced the presence of the Divine as I had never experienced God before. It seemed as though I could hear the quiet assurance of an inner voice saying: "Stand up for justice, stand up for truth; and God will be at your side forever." Almost at once my fears began to go. My uncertainty disappeared. I was ready to face anything.[2]

Dr. King had a renewed realization that the fight for justice and reconciliation requires a real dependence on the Holy Spirit and that prayer is a conversation with God. It is a dialogue and not a monologue, which means that we talk to God, but we also wait and we *listen* to hear what God will say to us. Our activism and our doing come out of our communion with God, as we remember who we are and acknowledge our powerful connection to an almighty God.

I imagine that Esther, like Dr. King, had a moment of realization while she was in her time of prayer. I suppose she too felt inadequate to go before the king to seek justice for her people. I wonder what inner voice resonated in her spirit. Trying to decide how to proceed was, no doubt, beyond her human comprehension. Racialization and violence are built on degrading historical narratives; resisting this dehumanization requires a completely new imagination built on new stories. This ability to see a different way forward is what Mennonite scholar John Paul Lederach calls "the creative third option." This mindset infuses us with hope, which allows us to challenge structures and systems by refusing to give in to the either/or options presented to us. It also enables us to choose creative ways to resist systemic injustice. So often, we only see one or two options: A or B, this or that. At first Esther probably saw only two options for herself: speak up or don't speak up; go to the king or keep yourself safe. But there is almost always a third option, and prayer provided the space for Esther to see that there was another creative way forward.

Prayer gives us God's perspective. It moves us past our knee-jerk reactions and helps us submit to the will and the way of God. Prayer cultivates patience. Prayer aligns us in an intimate partnership with God and others. That's why it's vital to recognize that Esther demonstrates the importance of prayer and discernment in community. She did not pray alone—she asked Mordecai to have the community join her and her handmaidens in prayer, united together. I often say that reconciliation cannot be done in isolation; it must be done in community. Having others who will listen to God with us, who may be able to corroborate what we feel and sense we're hearing from God in prayer, is essential. We can't do this alone!

In addition, when we pray, we are connected with a vision and a purpose that is higher than our own. Like Dr. King, in prayer we get a moral imagination of what God is doing and a vision of what we must do in response. I came to understand this in a life-changing way when I found myself in need of deep spiritual renewal after the 2016 presidential election of Donald Trump. I drove up to Sumas, Washington, for a two-day retreat to be alone with God. I was there during the Advent season, and when I turned to the Scripture passage in my devotional for that day, it was Matthew 11:3. As I read John the Baptist's questions to Jesus in that verse, "Are you the one we should be looking for? Or must we wait for someone else?" I began to weep uncontrollably. I was literally a mess! Something about his question seemed to sum up all the doubt and despair I felt about the election at a level that I couldn't articulate.

As a person who had devoted my whole life to the ministry of reconciliation and bringing people together, I was devastated by the result of the election! This was not upsetting to me because of who lost; I was heartbroken because of what message won. For decades, I poured myself out on behalf of the church because I wholeheartedly believed the message of reconciliation I preached. So when over 80 percent of white voting evangelicals[3] voted for a presidential candidate who degraded women, people of color, immigrants, and people with disabilities, while at the same time espousing white supremacist, nationalistic ideology, I was heartbroken! How could I reconcile this? I began to doubt whether my calling was worth it.

After I cried my eyes out, I wiped my tears and continued to read the Scripture. Just a few verses later, it said, "From the time of John the Baptist until now, violent people have been trying to take over the kingdom of heaven by force" (Matt. 11:12). Then I saw a vision of me charging the gates of hell, yelling and unafraid, with a spear in my hand. And I heard the Spirit say, "You will pierce the darkness with the leaders at the tip of the spear!" That experience changed my focus and gave birth to a new clarity and bravery in my life. I'm no longer trying to change all white evangelicals. My hope is to raise up a new generation of reconciliation leaders who will charge the gates of hell with me for the kingdom of God!

Through that prayer time, I received what Walter Brueggemann calls a "prophetic imagination." In his book by the same name, he identifies two key characteristics that define the role of the prophet: "*The task of prophetic ministry is to nurture, nourish, and evoke a consciousness and perception alternative to the consciousness and perception of the dominant culture around us.* . . . The alternative consciousness to be nurtured, on the one hand, serves to *criticize* in dismantling the dominant consciousness. . . . On the other hand, that alternative consciousness to be nurtured serves to *energize* persons and communities by its promise of another time and situation toward which the community of faith may move."[4] It was also through the power of prayer that Dr. King received his prophetic imagination. Not long after his kitchen table experience with God, he gave his famous "I Have a Dream" speech. In it he said, "I may not get there with you, but we as a people will get to the Promised Land!" He was so confident in what he'd seen from God about the future that he could unwaveringly energize the imaginations of all who have heard that message for generations since then.

Now my prophetic vision makes more sense. I will pierce the darkness of racism and injustice with the leaders whom I will influence and nurture and encourage in their practice of what I believe reconciliation really means: repairing broken systems together. This is a vision much larger and more difficult to accomplish than just having a song in Spanish during your church service or hosting a multicultural potluck once a year. That's why I'm being much more selective about the platforms and pulpits from which I speak and preach. I am no longer allowing myself to be used by ministries and organizations that are not truly committed to justice. I am done talking about diversity in terms of lofty platitudes, but I am determined to say the hard things and speak the difficult truths that are necessary in order for true reconciliation to occur. I am talking about the dismantling of the very structures of inequality and injustice. This approach to reconciliation requires a prophetic imagination, fervent prayer, and unwavering bravery. This vision came to me through prayer, and more prayer is needed to accomplish it.

Prayer gives us a vision and purpose greater than ourselves, and the courage to continue to confront social and political powers of injustice. It is through prayer that we receive the courage to embody God's heart for reconciliation and justice—to stand boldly, preach powerfully, and confront consistently because God through prayer has given us a vision of what is to come! We get a prophetic imagination or vision of what the future will entail. We may not know when or how, but we are confident that it will happen. Prayer has the power to transform systems, structures, and human beings in ways that we could not even think to ask or imagine.

When we pray, we affirm that justice and *shalom* are in God's hands. We acknowledge that there is a God who is above us and behind us and before us and within us. When we pray, we acknowledge that we need God in every area of our lives, no matter who were are: we might have a PhD, we might run marathons, we might be tough as nails, we might even be queen, but prayer is our chance to unequivocally communicate with God and remind ourselves that we cannot do the important work of reconciliation without God's help. Our activism comes out of our dependence on the Holy Spirit and is rooted in our understanding of the sovereignty of God. We are no match for the unseen realms of the spiritual world, but once we tap into the unlimited power of God just as those women did in Liberia, governments can be toppled. Similarly, Dr. King garnered the strength to lead the Montgomery bus boycott, which changed the course of the civil rights movement.

The brave people who participated in the civil rights marches believed in the paradoxical idea that positive transformation could be born of death. They nurtured their prophetic vision and imagination in community, where they built the collective faith and strength to believe that change was possible. They embodied this belief as they marched together, linking arms, declaring with every step, "We shall overcome!" It is on the shoulders of these brave people that we are now called to take our prophetic place in history. So I echo the words of my dear friend and spiritual daughter Austin Channing Brown, who proudly affirms in her book *I'm Still Here*, "I stand in the legacy of all that Black Americans have already accomplished—in their resistance, in their teachings, in their voices, in their faith—and I work toward a world unseen, currently unimaginable."[5] This is what we are called to do and what prayer enables us to believe is possible.

ELEVEN

SPEAKING TRUTH TO POWER

Then, even though it's against the law, I will go to the king; and
if I am to die, then die I will.

Esther 4:16 (CEB)

I REMEMBER exactly when God called me to devote
my life to the ministry of racial reconciliation. I was living
in Chicago and had recently started a religious organization
called Overflow Ministries. As a newly formed Christian
nonprofit, we needed to develop a reliable fundraising strategy to sustain our work. So I hired a person I knew from my
campus ministry days, someone who had years of experience working with Christian nonprofit companies, to help
me develop this new funding model. When he came to my
office to meet with my board, he sat at my desktop computer
and carefully studied our website. After a while, he swiveled
around, looked me straight in the eyes, and said, "I knew

we were starting something new, but I had no idea we were also conducting a funeral."

What? A funeral? I thought to myself. *Who's dying?* I had no idea what he was talking about! Then he explained that I was spread entirely too thin. He told me that everyone had a different idea of what my ministry was about. He was accurate in his critique and observed, "Some people think that you're a women's ministry, an evangelistic ministry, a college ministry, a marriage ministry, or a reconciliation ministry—and they're all right!" Then he said, "You can't raise money for a ministry that is this difficult to define." He encouraged me to focus all my energy on one issue—racial reconciliation. No more talks about gender. No more talks on spiritual gifts. Instead, he challenged me to let it all go and make racial reconciliation the sole focus of my ministry.

I was terrified. I listened to what he said but then immediately shook my head. No! No way. I can't do that! It would kill my ministry. Nobody would hire me. I might get a speaking engagement or two around the Martin Luther King Jr. holiday or Black History Month, but that would probably be it. I thought that if I did what he was suggesting, my ministry would be doomed, and there was *no* way I was going to destroy my work before it even got started. I had worked too hard for it! So, completely stunned, I decided to enter into a thirty-day period of prayer and discernment to determine whether I should take this extremely risky course of action.

During that time, I talked to many people, including chaplains who had invited me to speak on their college campuses. One of them agreed with me that most Christian colleges and universities did not focus on the topic of racial reconciliation throughout the year and that I would probably limit my opportunities to speak. However, the conversation that affected me the most was with a former InterVarsity Christian Fellowship colleague who said, "Don't do it, Brenda! Every person I've ever known who has made racial reconciliation the sole focus of their ministry has wound up dead!" He told me he was afraid I would *die* if I turned my focus to reconciliation. His fear was palpable. He was afraid for my life. Nevertheless, he paused and said, "But I don't know anyone who has been more called to do this than you."

This is the terrifying space that Esther now finds herself in. After Mordecai makes her aware of the dire situation facing the Jews, her first reaction is to say, "No! I can't do that! I could get in trouble. The king hasn't called me to come to him for thirty days. I can't go into the king's presence uninvited. It's against the law! I could lose my position—I could lose my life!"

Esther is right. Civil disobedience is scary! Refusing to comply with certain laws or to pay taxes and fines as a peaceful form of political protest can have terrible consequences. Our acts of nonviolent resistance can be misinterpreted as a rejection of the system of law as a whole. People will question our patriotism and respect for authority. Others will malign our character. Although morally correct in their opposition to injustice, those who engage in civil disobedience will face the legal consequences of their actions and perhaps the consternation of family and friends who disagree with their stance.

However, like Esther, we cannot stand idly by. Mordecai tells the queen that if she chooses to keep silent at a time such as this, relief and deliverance will come from some other place. In other words, God will use somebody else. Mordecai makes it clear to Esther and to us that God's kingdom will come on earth as it is in heaven—with or without our help. The only question is whether we will have the privilege of being a part of what God is doing. That could be why Mordecai says to Esther, almost as an afterthought, "Who knows? Perhaps you've been called to the kingdom for such a time as this." Mordecai seems to be suggesting that maybe everything Esther went through—all the hurt and the pain, the circumstances of her life, her adoption, her education, her beauty, her age, her faith, her bilingual skills—prepared her for this unique moment in history.

My former colleague was in essence asserting that perhaps I, like Esther, was created for such a time as this. And I wonder whether this extends to all of us today. Could it be that we are called to God's kingdom at this strategic time in history for a greater purpose? It is important to recognize when we are in the midst of significant times occurring in human history. When we identify these times, we must act decisively because windows of opportunity like this do not last indefinitely. They demand a response!

"The world will not be destroyed by those who do evil," Nobel Prize winner Albert Einstein once said, "but by those who watch them without doing anything."[1] Like Esther, we do not have the luxury of standing idly by when faced with the reality of injustice and inequality. We cannot wring our hands and hope for the best. We must take a public stand and risk getting involved. This will require us to face our greatest fears about what might happen if we take a public position for equality, reconciliation, and justice. It will not be easy, but I have learned that Dr. Martin Luther King Jr.

was right when he said, "Faith is taking the first step even when you don't see the whole staircase." Courage, I believe, is fear that has said its prayers and moves forward anyway! Like Esther, we will have to speak truth to power when it comes time to seize our strategic moment. Our elected officials, Christian leaders, and organizational presidents and administrators hold the power to address the urgent situations that desperately concern and affect so many people. Issues like human trafficking, sex slavery, child labor, racial discrimination, gender inequality, gun violence, economic and environmental injustice, mass incarceration, immigration, and the extinction of people demand our attention and concern. For me, it means speaking truth to denominational leaders, church pastors, college administrators, and others.

As reconcilers, we should care that people are viewed as expendable or as a means to financial gain. Our government officials need to know about this. They cannot continue to turn a blind eye or pretend that they don't know what is going on. Likewise, they cannot pass laws for political gain that contain hidden clauses allowing for the destruction of people. They must be told that someone in their administration or some lobbyist, perhaps someone like Haman, has been given enough authority to pass a law. Even if they, like King Xerxes, have given their consent to something they don't understand the full implications of, this does not absolve them of responsibility. They have sanctioned it and given permission for it to take place because it seemed politically expedient or was tied to something else they wanted.

How many government officials have benefited from the bribes, the kickbacks, and the promises to look the other way, to pretend they don't see what's going on and be blissfully ignorant regarding the destruction and devastation of people? That's why we must speak truth to power—to amplify the voices of those whose lives are being threatened. Leymah Gbowee, a prayerful social activist from Liberia, understands the power and significance of this sacred work. She says, "The one thing I have never been afraid of is standing before important people and speaking my mind. I represent women who may never have the opportunity to go to the United Nations or meet with a president. I'm never afraid to speak truth to power."[2]

That's why a group of ecumenical pastors and theologians in Soweto, South Africa, chose to publish a declaration called the Kairos Document in 1985. As Christian leaders, they felt compelled to speak out against the dehumanizing and vicious sociopolitical policies of apartheid. The document boldly proclaimed:

> The time has come. The moment of truth has arrived. South Africa has been plunged into a crisis that is shaking the foundations and there is every indication that the crisis has only just begun and that it will deepen and become even more threatening in the months to come. It is the KAIROS or moment of truth not only for apartheid but also for the Church. . . . We as a group of theologians have been trying to understand the theological significance of this moment in our history. It is serious, very serious. For very many Christians in South Africa this is the KAIROS, the moment of grace and opportunity, the favorable time in which God issues a challenge to decisive action. It is a dangerous time because, if this opportunity is missed, and allowed to pass by, the loss for the Church, for the Gospel and for all the people of South Africa will be immeasurable.[3]

So now, we too must find our courage to speak truth to those in power around us. Esther serves as an example for how to bravely deal with political powers, judicial leaders, government officials, college administrators, CEOs, and denominational hierarchy as we pursue reconciliation and equity for all people. She understands what is really at stake, so she chooses to face her fears and summon her courage, even if it means breaking the law, to confront the political powers of her day to help save people's lives.

Esther knew that going to the king was risky. She knew what had happened to the queen before her, and she knew what was about to happen to the Jewish people. There were no guarantees for Esther. Being the queen did not grant her automatic immunity. When her cousin implored her to speak up for her people, she balked—as any one of us would have. But after prayer and on further reflection, she decided to speak up. She finally said, "If I perish, I perish" (4:16 NIV). She decided to join in God's reparative work in the world, knowing full well that there were no promises that everything would turn out okay. And that's exactly what we're being asked to do too.

This reminds me of a lesson I learned about counting the cost of following Jesus. I was at Fuller Theological Seminary with two other graduate students, Peter and Mark, both from Singapore. We were talking about leading people to Christ. In response to their questions about my own process, I said that when I finish preaching, I invite people to receive Jesus as their Lord and Savior by praying a simple prayer with me. After listening carefully, they both said that they would never do that. I thought to myself, *Why not? As a minister, if you know a person wants to give their life to Jesus Christ, you should seal the deal immediately!*

So I asked them what they would do. They said that if a person hears the gospel and makes a decision that same night, without sincerely counting the cost of what it will mean for them, they advise him or her to go home and seriously consider the consequences of what this decision might mean. They went on to say, "If you still want to follow Jesus, even if your family disowns you or the government arrests you, then come back and we'll lead you to Jesus." Wow! I had never thought about it this way. In that moment I realized that we don't prepare people well for the obstacles and the opposition they may face for representing Jesus Christ and his kingdom.

There are no guarantees when it comes to being followers of Jesus who advocate for reconciliation. To be honest, I cannot guarantee that if you speak out for justice and fight with the whole of your life for reconciliation, things will turn out well for you. They might not. You could lose your job or your reputation. You might lose friendships or family members or your respectable standing in your community. You might not be popular in your workplace. You might feel isolated and alone and discouraged more often than not. You might put yourself in danger. You might even lose your life. I cannot guarantee that things will go well.

When I left my time with my former InterVarsity colleague, I was scared and more confused than ever. I fasted and prayed, but I was already starting to feel it: the prodding of the Holy Spirit to move forward. And then I heard these words from Esther rise up in my soul: "If I perish, I perish." It was then that I decided to take the risk to shift my focus and accept the call. I had no idea whether I would ever get another consulting or speaking job again. I didn't know whether my life would be in danger. I didn't know whether people would marginalize and pigeonhole me as a person who could only speak on one topic. But I listened to that still, small voice telling me which direction to walk—and the rest is history.

This decision is one that each of us must make as people committed to pursuing reconciliation. We are called to work with those who seek liberty and justice for all. God's kingdom is coming on earth, and we've been invited to get involved. Our fears and shortcomings may cause us to question our readiness to accept this invitation by asking, "Who, *me?*" But in response, God says, "Yes, *you*! Unlikely you, unprepared you, inexperienced you, uneducated you, teenage you, female you, divorced you, gay you, senior citizen you, housewife you, retired you, rich you, poor you, college student you, recovering addict you, dysfunctional family you!" In answer to the question, "Who, *me?*" God says, "Yes, *you!*"

So let us move forward guided by the words of educator and civil rights activist W. E. B. Du Bois, who was an agnostic for much of his life but nonetheless wrote dozens of exquisite spiritual entreaties. In the following prayer, he recalls Queen Esther, who daringly confronts her husband, King Xerxes, and demands that he overturn his court's order to kill all the Jews of the Persian Empire. It is with this prayer in mind—"Give Us Grace," written by Du Bois—that I prayerfully call us to go into the world as brave agents of reconciliation for such a time as this.

Give us grace, O God, to dare to do the deed which we well know cries to be done. Let us not hesitate because of ease, or the words of men's mouths, or our own lives. Mighty causes

are calling us—the freeing of women, the training of children, the putting down of hate and murder and poverty—all
these and more. But they call with voices that mean work and
sacrifice and death. Mercifully grant us, O God, the spirit of
Esther, that we say: I will go unto the King and if I perish,
I perish.[4]

TWELVE

THE RECONCILING POWER OF WOMEN

Three days later, Esther dressed in her royal robes and went to the inner court of the palace in front of the throne. The king was sitting there, facing the open doorway. He was happy to see Esther, and he held out the gold scepter to her.

When Esther came up and touched the tip of the scepter, the king said, "Esther, what brings you here? Just ask, and I will give you as much as half of my kingdom."

Esther answered, "Your Majesty, please come with Haman to a dinner I will prepare for you later today."

The king said to his servants, "Hurry and get Haman, so we can accept Esther's invitation."

Esther 5:1–5

AYELET WALDMAN was in the same class at Harvard Law School as President Barack Obama. She became a federal public defender and served in this capacity for a few years before becoming a writer and novelist. But her primary sense of identity is rooted in her Jewishness. Born in Jerusalem, she grew up in the United States but returned to Israel year after year during high school and college and planned to someday move there permanently. "For most of my life," she said in a 2016 interview on Public Radio International's "The World" news program, "I loved Israel, I longed for Israel, I planned to live in Israel."[1]

However, as Waldman's political and social consciousness blossomed and expanded beyond her own circles, she came to realize that the Israeli treatment of Palestinians did not sit well with her. Despite this, however, she did nothing. She didn't think there was anything she could do. Yet she never felt completely comfortable. Then, during a 2014 visit to Jerusalem for a writers' conference, everything changed for Ayelet. She visited Hebron, a city where criminally behaving Israeli settlers live among Palestinians in an urban context. She saw firsthand and up close what a military occupation looks like. She got proximate to the reality of the crippling injustice and did not like what she saw.

I can relate to her experience. In 2017, I too visited Israel-Palestine. While there, I learned about the 555 checkpoints, most of which are in Hebron and East Jerusalem. The checkpoints make it extremely difficult for Palestinians to do simple things like commute to work or to access or receive goods and services—including something as vital as an ambulance in an emergency. On the day I visited Hebron, I had to go through a checkpoint, which at first glance seems something like a security screening at an airport, with metal detectors and trained personnel. But these checkpoints are different in that they are fenced in, and only a certain number of people can fit into that space at a time. A gate at the front and back of the enclosure allows armed soldiers to let people out one-by-one to go through the screening process. When I entered the enclosed area, I immediately felt claustrophobic and anxiously said to myself, "I can't breathe!"

In that moment, my mind instantly remembered that these were also the last words of Eric Garner before he died of a chokehold by police officers in New York. All of a sudden, I felt an affinity with the plight, the suffering, and the oppression of the Palestinian people. I realized that they are being discriminated against and treated like second-class citizens, just like Black people in America, who are being killed in the street by police officers with no accountability or justice. This is traumatizing for people of color in the United States, and it is traumatizing for the Palestinian people. Everybody knows this is happening, but nobody seems to do anything about it. As a result, we feel like sitting ducks who can be shot and killed at will, which I imagine is exactly how the Palestinians feel. Where is the international community's condemnation of this? Why are they silent?

Ayelet Waldman decided that she would no longer keep quiet. Ultimately, she came home and realized that she would have to speak out. She no longer had a choice. She would have to speak out against the injustice and the violence and the pain that she witnessed. She also knew that it would come at a great cost. She knew that she would lose friends. She knew that she would lose much of her readership, which is composed predominantly of American Jewish women. She knew that she would probably be ostracized and alienated by her community. She knew this. But you know what? She did it anyway! She took a risk and spoke out. When asked why, her response was this: "My parents raised me on this concept, this Hebrew concept called *tikkun olam*, which means to fix the world. And you don't fix the world without personal risk."

After listening to her interview, I did more research and learned that the phrase *tikkun olam* (pronounced tee-KOON oh-LAHM) literally means "repair of the world." Within Orthodox and other Jewish interpretive communities, *tikkun olam* is interpreted as an aspiration for humanity to behave and act in partnership with God by taking steps to improve the state of the world through helping others. By so doing, we simultaneously bring more honor to God and establish God's sovereignty over the world. In the modern era, *tikkun olam* has come to connote social action, community service, and social justice. It suggests that Jews bear responsibility not only for their own moral, spiritual, and material welfare but also for the welfare of society. It has essentially become synonymous with the notion of social action, justice, and the pursuit of social change.

Waldman knew what time it was, and she cared enough to speak up and get involved. "You don't fix the world without personal risk." That's the truth! Our calling to speak out and break our silence about injustice, to raise our voice for the voiceless, and to take a stand against oppression and systems that weaken and abuse others will always involve personal risk. That is a hard reality to face, but, try as we might, there's just no way around it! Reconciliation requires us to care, and that's risky, and it takes a great deal of courage to pursue it.

Now it is Esther's turn to find the courage to speak truth to power. This is what author Ada María Isasi-Díaz describes, in her book *Mujerista Theology*, as the declaration of women to assert themselves in conversations to which they have not been invited by saying, *"Permítanme hablar"*—"Permit me to speak."[2] In other words, "I have something to say!" As Esther moves forward by faith, she will discover that she is not just a mousy little girl who happened to win a beauty contest, but that she is, in fact, a warrior. All of the struggles, heartache, and adversity she has been through have proven that she is a woman who is brave and stronger than she thinks.

After seeking God's face and fasting for three days, Esther knows what she must do. She has a strategy. She puts on her royal robes, adorning herself with her adopted cultural identity in hopes of connecting with the king, and rushes into the royal chamber. Yes, she is breaking the law, but she shows a certain degree of deference by dressing in a way that respects the cultural norms of her context. It's enough, at least, to get her through the door. And now that she has the king's attention, he asks her why she has come so unexpectedly to his chambers. There must be something urgent and of great importance that has caused her to risk her life to get his consideration.

At this point Esther, like Waldman, is embarking on her shero's journey. A "shero" is a female hero who displays strong heroic traits under tremendous pressure and who triumphs over her circumstances. She is an example of what is possible, a brilliant inspiration to people of all ages. Although women are often viewed as the "weaker vessel," the shero's journey reveals the truth that God created women as warriors from the beginning. The Hebrew word *ezer* offers a glimpse into the full truth of this. Used twice in Genesis to describe the first woman, Eve, as a "helper" or "helpmate" (as it is traditionally translated), *ezer* is used elsewhere in Scripture three times to refer to strong military forces and sixteen times to refer to God. When we look at its Hebrew origins, we find that it is a combination of two roots, one meaning "to rescue" or "to save" and the other meaning "to be strong." Clearly, then, the full meaning of *ezer* is much more powerful than the traditional "helper" interpretation. How often have we thought of women as being strong people who save others? How different would the world be if we did? There is certainly dignity in helping, but Scripture teaches that women are more than helpers. A woman is a person of great strength and power. She is a warrior, made in the image of God.

In her book *Love Warrior*, Glennon Doyle describes the modern-day warrior woman like this:

> I think about the tragedies the women in my life have faced. How every time a child gets sick or a man leaves or a parent dies or a community crumbles, the women are the ones who carry on, who do what must be done for their people in the midst of their own pain. While those around them fall away, the women hold the sick and nurse the weak, put food on the table, carry their families' sadness and anger and love and hope. They keep showing up for their lives and their people with the odds stacked against them and the weight of the world on their shoulders. They never stop singing songs of truth, love, and redemption in the face of hopelessness. They are inexhaustible, ferocious, relentless co-creators with God, and they make beautiful worlds out of nothing. Have women been the Warriors all along?[3]

This clearer understanding of the role of women in society is why it's so vital to empower them! There's a truism in global development circles that says, "Educate a woman and you educate a nation." In other words, when women are educated, their communities will also prosper. Sadly, the converse is also true: if we deny women access to education, the world will suffer. Most people know that educating boys *and* girls, men *and* women, is morally right, and I applaud all efforts to do so. When we educate girls and women, the benefits are felt throughout the whole community. This positive relationship between *female* education in particular and the overall outcomes for community development has been well documented. By participating in the labor market, an educated woman helps boost economic productivity, leading to greater wealth for her community. In addition, an educated woman's household is more likely to flourish because of her higher income. When we empower women and girls, we empower all those around them for generations to come.[4]

We see this all over the world as women are speaking up and demanding that their voices and concerns be heard. This is not just for themselves but for the sake of the world around them. Tawakkol Abdel-Salam Karman is one such woman. She is a Yemeni journalist, politician, and human rights activist. This brave warrior leads the group Women Journalists Without Chains. She worked tirelessly for justice on behalf of her people during the 2011 Yemeni uprising that was part of the Arab Spring revolts. Some Yemenis call her the "Iron Woman" and "Mother of the Revolution." The world has taken note of her courageous fight for peace, justice, equality, and reconciliation. In 2011, she was the corecipient of the Nobel Peace Prize, becoming the first Arab woman to win a Nobel Prize.[5]

Esther certainly knows the incredible amount of bravery it takes to serve one's people as the mother of a revolution. In response to the king's question about why she has abruptly come into his chambers, she invites his royal highness and Haman to please come and eat with her. But wait. *That's* her grand plan to save her people from destruction—to have a dinner party? I don't know about you, but that certainly doesn't sound like a great strategy to me. But maybe Esther knows something more about the profound truth that the simple act of eating together represents.

I recently spoke with a dear friend who reminded me of the radically subversive nature of eating together. She is an African American woman who married a white man not long ago. They were united in a beautiful, intimate destination wedding and, now that they've returned home, they are having a large reception for their friends and family. But they realized that most of their family and friends would meet each other for the first time at this event! Tensions also grew as the cultural gap between these two communities became more painfully apparent. As we talked, lamented, and prayed about the situation, I remembered the sacred symbolism of eating together. We decided that perhaps this reception could be a place to affirm the common humanity and dignity of all people present by sharing a meal together.

The reverse of this was true for enslaved Black people, who were allowed to cook and serve food to their White masters but were absolutely forbidden to eat that food at the same table. The visually potent act of eating together would demonstrate a truth that was unimaginable and intolerable for White people to affirm. Langston Hughes, the renowned African American poet of the Harlem Renaissance, describes this reality in his iconic poem "I, Too."[6] The speaker in the poem begins by declaring that he too is an American. He is claiming his right to feel patriotic toward America, despite how he is mistreated as a Black man in this country. He asserts this even though he is the "darker" brother who cannot sit at the table and must eat in the kitchen. This alludes to the common practice of racial segregation during the early twentieth century, when African Americans faced discrimination in nearly every aspect of their lives. We were forced to live, work, eat, and travel separately from our White counterparts, had few civil or legal rights, were often victims of racial violence, and faced economic discrimination and marginalization in both the North and the South.

Eating together is a practice that humanizes people by acknowledging and affirming that we all hunger for the same things. Whether we are rich or poor, black or white, male or female, gay or straight, indigenous or immigrant, we all need food and water. In the subtle but subversive act of eating together, we recognize and uphold the truth that what one person hungers for is ultimately what all people hunger for. It embodies the common human bond between us, admitting that your needs are also my needs. In doing this, we recognize that we are all made in the image of God and are worthy of being treated with dignity and respect. This is why White people refused to let their slaves eat with them. They could not bear the fact that they all were equally made in the image of God, regardless of race, gender, social class, nationality, or any other human distinctive.

I recently saw this truth demonstrated by a group of graduate students at Seattle Pacific University. They were alarmed when they learned that the hiring process for two tenured faculty positions excluded student participation and did not include any candidates of color. In response, they wrote and circulated a petition demanding that the search process be stopped. They wanted a new search to be launched so that two people of color could be hired for the open positions. The university, they explained, had vowed to give them a culturally diverse academic education, and they expected the institution to deliver on that promise.

Some of their professors and fellow students were deeply hurt by and upset about the petition. To help quell the tensions and foster reconciliation, the students hosted a potluck for the faculty and their student peers. Gathering together around a meal was more than just a thoughtful gesture. The students, as Christians, wanted to create an atmosphere that affirmed God's presence with us in community and modeled a way forward rooted in equitable partnership. So they chose a familiar church practice that revolved around their commonality as people and the religious tradition of breaking bread together. It demonstrated their commitment to reconciliation and emphasized their communion in the midst of struggle. Afterward, students and faculty alike said that the meal helped to quiet some of their anxiety and fear. People embraced, and their hearts became more open toward one another. This is the humanizing power of eating a meal together—and perhaps it's what Queen Esther was trying to do for the nemesis of her people, Haman.

King Xerxes and Haman come happily to dine with Esther, and during the meal the king asks Esther what he can give her. He offers her half the kingdom—whatever she wants. And what does Esther say she wants? "Come again tomorrow" (Esther 5:7–8). I'm guessing that even Esther didn't have the full plan in her mind when she set out to ask the king and Haman to dine with her. I'm guessing she only knew what first step she ought to take and was relying on God to reveal what she needed to know as she went.

This approach to confronting those in power reminds me of a very insightful training I attended, led by Rev. Alexia Salvatierra, a Lutheran pastor and former director of justice ministries for the Southwest California Synod of the ELCA (Evangelical Lutheran Church in America). She is also the coauthor, with Peter Heltzel, of *Faith-Rooted Organizing: Mobilizing the Church in Service to the World*. In this book, they stress that Christian advocacy involves asking governments "to do what God has called government to do." They firmly believe that Christian advocacy must combine what they call "serpent power" and "dove power."[7] In her seminar, Reverend Salvatierra explained this in more detail by sharing the teachings of Jesus in Matthew 10:16: "Behold, I send you forth as sheep in the midst of wolves: be ye therefore wise as serpents, and harmless as doves" (KJV). As she expounded on this text, she clarified that in order for people of faith to engage in social action, if we really want to see change, we must employ both general political tactics and Christianity-specific strategies.

The first approach, which she calls "serpent power," includes typical political mechanisms like laws, elections, negotiation, constituency representation, op-eds, and direct action. However, as Christ-followers we have deep resources in our faith that our organizing activities must also be rooted in. For that reason, when Christians get involved in activism and advocacy, we must also use what Salvatierra calls "dove power." This unseen force is able to turn enemies into friends through faith and love. When Christians use this approach, we are able to bring prophetic vision to our advocacy, which helps people remember who they are and inspires them to work to achieve their dreams. "There is no greater gift," Salvatierra said in our seminar, "than to help someone be the person that God has called them to be." By coming alongside those making decisions about matters of justice and human flourishing, we have the opportunity to contribute our distinct perspective in a nonthreatening way that might influence a leader to do the right thing because we show them that we care about them. This is the subversive influence of being "harmless as doves." It could be that, by inviting Haman and the king to dinner, Esther was using her dove power as she symbolically reminded these political leaders of their shared humanity with her.

After the first dinner, Haman and the king both left in good spirits. But once again, Haman was angered because Mordecai would not bow before him. In his anger, Haman ordered that a gallows be made, and he arranged to hang Mordecai the following day. This form of public execution was intended not only to frighten the obstinate Mordecai but also to instill a sense of fear in the entire Jewish community. The gallows served as a visible symbol of intimidation and fear, much like lynchings were symbols of terrorism by White-dominant culture, intended to instill fear in the hearts and minds of Black people. The brutal act of leaving the dead, mutilated bodies of men, women, and children swinging from trees like some kind of "strange fruit" was a statement to all Black people of the perpetual threat of violence that lurked around them if they dared to act outside socially established norms.

The conscious and unconscious psychological purpose of this type of threat is to create an overwhelming sense of fear and insecurity for the disadvantaged in the face of the socially and politically strong. Ultimately, its goal is the death of the self. In this environment of personal and social insecurity, all hope, all dreams, and all ambitions die and are replaced with a sense of defeat, which is one of the greatest tragedies of the disinherited. In his book *Jesus and the Disinherited*, theologian, philosopher, and civil rights activist Howard Thurman makes this clear.

> The threat of violence within a framework of well-nigh limitless power is a weapon by which the weak are held in check. Artificial limitations are placed upon them, restricting freedom of movement, of employment, and of participation in the common life. . . . The threat of violence may be implemented not only by constituted authority but also by anyone acting in behalf of the established order. Every member of the controllers' group is in a sense a special deputy, authorized by the mores to enforce the pattern. This fact tends to create fear, which works on behalf of the proscriptions and guarantees them. The anticipation of possible violence makes it very difficult for any escape from the pattern to be effective.[8]

As Thurman rightly observes, "Fear is one of the persistent hounds of hell that dog the footsteps of the poor, the dispossessed, and the disinherited."[9] But there is an antidote to the threat of violence. As Mordecai and Esther will discover, the key to unlocking the door of our individual and corporate hopes for the future is believing that we are made in the image of God and that an unseen force is working on our behalf. Haman was stopped short of executing Mordecai because the king recalled, that same night, how Mordecai had previously

saved him from an assassination plot. He ordered that Mordecai be honored by all and paraded on horseback in the king's
royal robes. What are the odds that this would happen the
night before he was to be executed? What may appear to be
serendipity might actually be sovereignty—God being active
in human affairs, intervening on behalf of the people of God.

The king's actions in pulling out the chronicles and being
reminded that Mordecai saved his life give us insight into the
mysterious reality of divine intervention. On the night before
Haman planned to kill him, the king has insomnia, calls for
the public records, and reads about how Mordecai saved his
life and was not honored for it. The conspiracy to kill the
king was insider information that was not supposed to be
shared with anyone, especially not with a Jew like Mordecai
or with a woman like Esther. Typically, people in the majority
culture control information and use it to their advantage. But
in this case, either the conspirators were careless and it cost
them their lives, or the unseen God was at work—or both!
Either way, Mordecai "accidentally" overhears the plot to
assassinate the king, which later prompts the king to honor
the Jewish man who saved his life—on the night before the
man was to be publicly executed!

After Mordecai's life was spared, the king and Haman
went to the second banquet prepared for them by Queen
Esther. King Xerxes again offered his queen anything she
desired, up to half his kingdom. Did you catch that Esther
didn't answer the king until he asked her three times? This
makes me smile as I think of the cultural implications. In the
Western world, our direct culture usually expects an answer
the first time. However, in this text's Eastern cultural context,
Xerxes was quite comfortable waiting two days and having

to ask three times to find out what his queen wanted. Finally, Esther was ready to respond.

> Queen Esther answered, "If I please the king, and if the king wishes, give me my life—that's my wish—and the lives of my people too. That's my desire. We have been sold—I and my people—to be wiped out, killed, and destroyed. If we simply had been sold as male and female slaves, I would have said nothing. But no enemy can compensate the king for this kind of damage."
>
> King [Xerxes] said to Queen Esther, "Who is this person, and where is he? Who would dare do such a thing?"
>
> Esther replied, "A man who hates, an enemy—this wicked Haman!" Haman was overcome with terror in the presence of the king and queen. (Esther 7:3–6 CEB)

Her request was simply that the king would spare her life and the lives of her people. What courage that request entailed though! After further pleading from Esther and conversations with both Esther and Mordecai, the king agreed to spare the Jews by allowing them to fight back on the day they were supposed to be annihilated, and Haman was hanged outside his own house on the gallows he had built for Mordecai.

At this point, I feel compelled to pause briefly to consider the fate of Haman. Hanging isn't exactly the rosy picture of reconciliation that I would like to paint. Hanging Haman appears, in fact, to be the opposite of reconciliation, so I would be remiss if I did not address it. The truth is, though, that I don't entirely know what to make of Haman's fate. Here is what I do know: As I've said previously, the ritual of breaking bread or sharing a meal is very important, and this is true in the Jewish community. Blessings are said at the start and end of the meal, food is shared, and eating itself is a sacred act. Jewish tradition sees a meal as a time for intimacy, fellowship, and significant conversation.[10] In giving Haman a chance to see her humanity, I think Esther was also giving him the opportunity to reaffirm and reclaim his own humanity in this intimate setting.

The belief that our humanity is interconnected is central to an ancient South African philosophy called Ubuntu. This term means "humanity to others" or "I am what I am because of who we all are." Ubuntu conveys that "I cannot fully become who God created me to be unless you become who God created and intended you to be." In other words, God created us to need each other to survive. We are meant to be nurtured in communities characterized by mutually affirming, interdependent relationships.

Archbishop Desmond Tutu called on Ubuntu theology to denounce apartheid and call for reconciliation and justice in South Africa. He urged South Africans to understand that when we dehumanize others, we also dehumanize ourselves. This is true not only in South Africa but in the United States and around the world. It is impossible to exploit or brutalize another human being without deadening something within one's self. Dr. John M. Perkins, the father of the Christian community development movement, saw this when he was tortured in a Mississippi jail. He describes it like this in his book *Let Justice Roll Down*:

When they started torturing us, it was horrifying, I couldn't even imagine that this was happening. One of the officers took a fork that was bent down and he brought that fork up to me and he said, "Have you seen this?," and he took that fork and put that fork into my nose, then he took that fork and pushed it down my throat. And then he took me over there and beat me to the ground. . . .

They were like savages—like some horror out of the night. And I can't forget their faces, so twisted with hate. It was like looking at white-faced demons. Hate did that to them. But you know, I couldn't hate them back. When I saw what hate had done to them, I couldn't hate back. I could only pity them. I didn't ever want hate to do to me what it had already done to those men.[11]

As I read of Haman's demise, I was struck by how he equated leadership with power. It seemed that his sole purpose for gaining the favor of the king was to extend his reach, solidify his reputation, and harm his enemies. Unfortunately, in my experience, many leaders share with Haman some version of those same flaws. But what makes Haman dangerous is that those were his *only* goals. When this happens, that's when leadership becomes a code word for power. By contrast, Xerxes had a blending of reasons for wanting to lead. Obviously, a king has a whole set of issues that we can't comprehend, but it seems obvious that he wanted to create a stable society with some rule of law. Yes, he wanted to secure his power and harm his enemies as he inflated his own reputation. But he also wanted to see justice done and people honored for their loyalty.

I truly believe that by inviting Haman to eat with her, Esther was creating space and allowing room for Haman to repent and move toward reconciliation. She does this not once but twice. Ultimately, although given ample opportunities, Haman chooses not to change. Instead, when given the opportunity to reclaim his humanity, he refused it. He continued with his plans to murder Mordecai and all the Jews, and this is what eventually led to his own demise. In his attempt to destroy others, Haman ultimately destroyed himself.

As reconcilers, we must know that each of us will have people in our lives who choose the path that leads *away* from reconciliation instead of toward it. We cannot force them to make different choices, but we can and should continue to provide the space for change and to press on in the hope that they will someday choose a better way. Reconciliation must always hold out hope for transformation to occur and provide the opportunity for people to repent. This is what is uniquely different about how we engage the work for justice and reconciliation from a Christian perspective. As followers of Christ, we believe that every person reflects the image of God and that our God is able to bring life out of death. This means that in our work for justice, there must always be a pathway to transformation for everyone. Reconciliation is not revenge. Instead, as Father Robert Schreiter accurately states, "Reconciliation makes of both victim and oppressor a new creation."[12] It is our creativity and prophetic imagination that give us the capacity to perceive things at a deeper level than what initially meets the eye. As a result, we are able to imagine ourselves in a web of relationships that includes even our enemies. This allows us to break out of what may appear to be narrow, shortsighted, or structurally determined dead ends. We are no longer bound by what existing views of perceived reality suggest or by what prescriptive answers determine is possible.

Unfortunately, still today there are influential leaders like Haman who are motivated by their xenophobic, competitive, and combative misuse of power for their own gain and self-aggrandizement. Therefore, I'm convinced that there is a need for the collaborative, community-building power of women, as demonstrated by Esther—power that works to counteract the divisive and destructive energy that is so pervasive in our world today. Women, especially women of color, must be encouraged and supported in positions of leadership. Our experience of oppression has given us clarity into how things must change. If we are really looking for reconciliation leaders, we must look among the marginalized, disenfranchised, and vulnerable in any society and culture because they are the ones who push, prod, and poke people to move toward equality and freedom.

Yes, Esther is an example of the reconciling power of women that we so desperately need in our world today. Like Queen Esther, women have decided to be brave and take our rightful place as the warriors that God has created us to be in order to help repair the world. Because of these sheroes, I pray that a new sense of unity and collaboration will emerge, leading to our collective survival. May women birth creative and subversive strategies that cultivate solidarity and communion rather than replicating the ego-driven, competitive approaches of the past. May we support their leadership, and may all of us find the courage to pursue racial justice, knowing that our collaboration has the potential to profoundly influence the credibility and clarity of what our reconciliation work must address now in repairing broken systems so all people are safe, cared for, and able to thrive.

CONCLUSION

Seizing Our Moment of Destiny

IN 2015, I went with other Christian leaders to Washington, DC, to lobby Congress for immigration reform. We walked the halls of our nation's capital and knocked on the doors of our government's leaders, asking them to lend their support to legislation that would repair our broken immigration system. I must admit that it was really scary. I was so intimidated. Not just because I would be talking to politicians, but because I was unsure how, exactly, I was supposed to go about it! There is a whole lingo involved with politics at that level, and I worried that I would not have the skills I needed to be persuasive.

Suppose someone asked me something about the bill for which I was so ardently lobbying, and I didn't have an answer? Suppose someone mentioned other laws and legislation, and I didn't know what they were talking about? I was worried that I would be exposed as a fraud. This was way outside my comfort zone, and I felt wholly inadequate for the task at hand. Here I was, just an ordinary citizen with no political clout whatsoever, in these massive buildings where the truly influential come to play. It was awe-inspiring, thrilling, and completely terrifying. Being in the epicenter of our nation's political playing field, where everything from the buildings to the grounds to the monuments served to show our nation's might and power, I felt especially small and powerless.

Perhaps Esther also felt this way when Mordecai challenged her to go to the king and speak truth to power because it was her time to act. Summoning her courage, she said, "Then I will go in to see the king, even if it means I must die." Likewise, we too have to conclude that it doesn't matter how we feel or whether we think we are ready. There are many important, life-threatening issues of injustice everywhere we look that need to be addressed: gun violence, mass incarceration, immigration, the exploitation of the elderly, racial disparities in our nation's enforcement of drug laws, daily microaggressions against people of color, economic and environmental injustice, and many more. If you don't see these injustices, then you're not paying attention! And so we, like Esther, must seize our moment of destiny and summon our courage to speak truth to those in power around us, even if it scares us to death! In the face of these huge social issues, we must resolve to make this world better for all people.

I came to that conclusion for myself when I returned to the United States after studying Spanish for the summer in Costa Rica. When I arrived, I noticed that there were two different customs lines to enter the country. One line was for nonresidents, and the other was for US citizens and Canadians. I was surprised to see how extremely diverse the

US line was! There were people who appeared to be from all over the world. Then I looked and saw that the same amount of diversity was true of those in the nonresident line. As I pondered this, I thought to myself, *We're already a diverse country. We have enough diversity*. Instantly, I felt like God put a check in my spirit. I heard God asking me three questions: "Do you believe that I love you and will supply your needs? Do you believe that I have enough resources for everybody? Do you believe that I want the same for others as I want for you?" And to all three of these questions I whispered under my breath, "Yes, Lord!"

In that moment, I realized that God was warning me about my scarcity thinking, an impulse that causes us to fear that there's not enough to go around—jobs, college tuition, food, housing, and so forth. As a result, our impulse is to keep all the "good stuff" for ourselves and to build walls to keep those "other" people out. Wow! That day, standing right there in the customs line, I had a revelation! I knew that those thoughts about having "enough diverse people" were not from God. As reconcilers, we cannot separate our concern for people from the policies that affect their lives, like immigration reform. Policies are rules or principles that guide decisions that affect people. For years, I've worked hard to speak Spanish fluently because I sincerely love and feel an affinity with Latina/o people. Because of my experience in that customs line when I returned from Costa Rica, I accepted the invitation to lobby Congress, knowing that I can't claim to love people and not care about the policies that negatively affect their lives.

That's why I will no longer focus on simply coming together as diverse ethnic groups. Instead, my goal is to activate reconcilers to repair broken systems that are rooted in the evil of racism and resist the kingdom of God. I will not hide behind the mask of niceness or pretend not to be angry in an effort to make White people feel more comfortable with my ministry of reconciliation. I will speak my truth. I will stand in truth, and I will no longer dumb down the truth to help White people feel less guilty. To do so is to be complicit in sanitizing the truth, and I refuse to be complicit in that any longer. Reconciliation happens by repairing broken systems and engaging power, not just by focusing on relationships and feelings.

So now it's your turn to become brave. Are you ready to get moving? Are you ready to take action? These issues of injustice, large and small, are demanding our attention. Are we willing to fight with and for others with no benefit to ourselves? Will we be a new expression of the church that is actively working to create equitable environments and advocate for the needs of marginalized people around the world? Will we partner with others to repair broken systems and structures so that all creation can flourish? As Mordecai said to Esther when she initially doubted whether she was up to the task, "And who knows but that you have come to your royal position for such a time as this?" (Esther 4:14 NIV). Maybe we too have come to the kingdom as people of faith for this particular time in history. A quote attributed to Sir Winston Churchill serves as a good reminder of this: "There comes a time in every person's life when they are given a unique opportunity to discover the purpose for which they were born. It is their moment of destiny. And if they seize it, it becomes their finest hour."

Perhaps this is our moment of destiny. Maybe if we risk seizing this strategic moment in history, it will become our finest hour as we take our prophetic place. To do that, I believe we must do specific work to (1) reclaim our identity and agency as people of color, (2) confront whiteness, (3) repair broken systems together, and (4) restore the credibility of the church.

1. Reclaim Our Identity and Agency as People of Color

Part of the impact of a racialized society on African Americans in the United States has been the deconstruction of our historical narrative and identity. However, our Christianity does not have to be a story about slave masters who converted us and about our finding Christ in spite of their cruelty. That is a metanarrative of God only working through whites that we must scrutinize and totally abandon. Based on this story, many reconciliation efforts are too focused on African Americans and people of color trying to convince White people to change and to take our concerns more seriously. As we move forward, we must reclaim our sense of agency, our story, and our rightful place in the world. Ours is a story that uniquely qualifies us to get involved in and lead the work of racial justice and reconciliation globally. There is a world waiting for our unique story and prophetic witness. To begin, we must reconnect to our history and our heritage and reaffirm our origins. One way to do this is through DNA testing.[1] This process is the beginning of restoring and reclaiming our narrative and identity as reconcilers. We can make a radical difference in the world as we understand there is a greater conversation for us to engage in.

I learned this when I went to Kenya for the first time. When I arrived, the customs agent asked me, "Is this your first time in Africa?" I said yes, and then he smiled and said, "Welcome home, Dada!" which means, "Welcome home, sister!" It was an indescribable feeling to be back on the continent from which my ancestors were stolen. During my visit, I was surprised how much Kenyans wanted to know about African Americans. Young girls touched my hair and felt my skin. I bartered for goods in the market with *Jet* and *Ebony* magazines because my people hungered to see positive images of African Americans. The negative stereotypes we received in the United States about Africans were similar to the toxic messages they received about us.

We can heal that. We can find a way for our bodies to get in the same place and have conversations that are not sanctioned by white evangelicals or anybody else! This means that our specific work requires decolonizing our own minds and seeing the ways we have bought into white supremacy. We must examine the ways that we buy into this racial hierarchy by being unwilling to sacrifice ourselves for other nonwhite people who face discrimination. We have often given our lives in hopes of saving or changing white people, but we weren't as willing to make those same sacrifices for our Latina/o, Native American, Vietnamese, Hmong, Palestinian, or Syrian brothers and sisters, even though they are seeking justice just as we are.

We must not take ourselves for granted. We can use our traditions, our resources, our fellowship, and our multiracial communities to sharpen one another, without needing white approval or support. We can talk about ways to galvanize and mobilize our common sense of connection. Rather than focusing our conversation on how to get white people to change, new questions could be: How can we stand with our

Latina/o sisters and brothers to fix immigration? How can we extend God's family to them? We have to ask new questions, global questions like, How can we care about Afro Brazilians? What could that explicit conversation be like? What could it lead to? What about the persecution of our Native American brothers and sisters and their fight for environmental justice? How can we stand with them? That's the critical perspective we must have in order to move beyond critique to providing a future vision of racial justice and reconciliation for people of color.

2. Confront Whiteness

For whites, it is impossible to fully internalize the concept of whiteness as being good. This produces guilt and shame that paralyzes, causing denial, silence, and inactivity regarding reconciliation and racial justice. Therefore, it is necessary to take the implications of whiteness more seriously. Instead of reconciliation being solely focused on getting to know and understand people of color, there must be a new focus for white people, one that is directed at understanding, unpacking, and confronting their own whiteness. Although we must all find our deepest sense of identity in Christ, those who are white can't get there without breaking free of the distorted sense of identity they've internalized from the narrative of racial difference. That's why whites who are committed to reconciliation need a new paradigm that takes the problem of whiteness more seriously. That will require doing the specific work of dealing with whiteness and its implications regarding their lack of engagement with racial justice and reconciliation.

It is deeply disturbing that so many Christians think that racial reconciliation is some kind of liberal, politically motivated social agenda that has nothing to do with their faith as followers of Jesus Christ. It is also an indictment of the church that so many Christians don't know that the gospel includes reconciliation across racial, gender, ethnic, social, and cultural barriers. Our call to discipleship is an invitation to follow Jesus into a new community. We are called to make disciples who create corporate, social change as part of a new community of people who love the Lord with all their heart, mind, soul, and strength and love their neighbor as themselves (Luke 10:27). Because whiteness has a negative impact on everyone living in a racialized society, it is crucial that white people do the brave work of confronting it.

3. Repair Broken Systems Together

I once hoped for a large reconciliation movement, but the truth is that reconciliation is contextual. It will look different in various places, depending on the context, with particular work for different people and communities to do. So where do we even begin? How do we start? I believe the best place to start is in your own backyard. Prayerfully consider your neighborhood. What schools are nearby? What are the health-care options? Do you live near a prison? Do you live in the suburbs? Ask God to show you the injustice that is nearest you. That's where we start! Some of us might find ourselves on a path like civil rights lawyer Bryan Stevenson's that will take us onto a national stage, engaging in national issues. Others of us might only make it as far as the school around the corner. But all of us can engage in God's work of reconciliation. In either case, know that these words by the great Catholic priest and theologian Henri Nouwen are true: "Those who choose, even on a small scale, to love in the midst of hatred and fear are the people who offer true hope to our world."[2]

This attempt to make the world a better place will not always be met with people's approval. We must become brave enough, like Esther, to face whatever the possible consequences are for being agents of reconciliation. That means we must work for reconciliation knowing that there are no guarantees. Theologian and author Dr. Willie James Jennings, a dear friend of mine, warns that the attempt to dominate and control through whiteness will not yield easily. He says, "All naïve expectations about some kind of easily achieved Shalom have to be in some way reordered, shattered, and left in disarray until sufficient quiet, agreement, and readiness together has been created, in order to necessarily come to a new future."[3]

The evidence all around us, in support of Jennings's warning, points to depravity and suffering. What I see when I look around are systems of oppression. What I see when I look around are men and women and children living with PTSD due to the weight of living in a racialized society.[4] I see black children like Tamir Rice shot on the playground by white police officers. I see white actors dressing up in "yellowface" to portray Asians.[5] I see vast wealth gaps stratified by race.[6] I see inequity in our schools, including gifted programs that are strongly skewed by race.[7] I see Native American women two and half times more likely to be sexually assaulted than any other women in the United States.[8] Most places I look I see darkness and despair.

In the face of these pressing social problems, we must demonstrate that reconciliation happens by repairing broken systems and confronting power, not just by focusing on relationships and feelings. Addressing systemic injustice will look different in each specific context. But change that truly matters will always manifest as tangible acts of justice that help people and communities thrive and flourish. This will require working together with people in your local community who are being adversely affected by unjust systems and structures. These people are the experts on what issues need to be addressed and what would really solve the problem. Start by asking, "Are there people in my community who remain unheard? Are there people who are being ignored because they make others uncomfortable because of their race, class, gender, mental illness, disability, sexuality, or other marginalized social status?" Maybe a practical way to repair broken systems with them would be to amplify their voices by voting in solidarity to make sure their needs and concerns are taken seriously. Another idea might be to stand with families in your community and advocate for education reform and better resources in the public school system. It could be that instead of just praying for those affected by mass incarceration in this country, your group could find ways to be involved with systemic policy change or help women and men get readjusted back into society. You could also work with others to start a community garden to address the lack of healthy options in "food deserts" in your city. Finally, you and your faith community could attend town hall meetings or community activist events to support the specific issues happening in your local context. These are only a few ideas of what it might mean to actively work together with others in your community to repair broken systems.

But, in spite of these realities, there is hope. I am not talking about a superficial or merely optimistic hope. I am not hoping in what I can see with just a cursory glance. Instead, I am hoping in what I cannot always see. I am hoping in a God of light and restoration and peace. I am hoping in a God who broke into this damaged world to offer us abundant life. I am hoping in a God who repairs broken systems. I cannot always see evidence of it, but I'm willing to act in spite of the evidence. I'm willing to believe that transformation is possible with God. I'm willing to believe that God is always at work among us, always inviting us into that reparative work.

4. Restore the Credibility of the Church

In my process of becoming brave, I have come full circle in my views about the church. I was so disappointed with the inability of Christians to effectively deal with the issue of racial injustice that I'd almost given up on the institutional church. Why was the church necessary when people who are not Christians seem to be doing a better job working for reconciliation and racial justice than we are? Why do they need us if we don't do a good job at it anyway? In many ways this is true, but I've come to the conclusion that we do need the church, ragtag army though we may be, because we've been entrusted with the transcendent narrative of faith that offers us hope and the possibility of transformation. That's why the church cannot abandon its leadership in the work of reconciliation. The message of the gospel, the story we must tell, infuses the work of reconciliation with *hope*! Without a story bigger than ourselves, as finite humans we fall into perpetual despair. However, rooted in a theology and narrative of hope, we are able to continue to resist and defy the odds that seem to be stacked against us.

As a Christian, I believe that out of death comes life. That is the narrative that we have in Jesus Christ. The promise and the paradox of the resurrection is that if you lose your life for the sake of the reconciling work of the gospel, you will find it. I can't promise that it will always be easy. I can't promise that you will be victorious in your pursuits on this side of heaven. But I can promise that God will bring life out of what you lose and will ultimately restore all things. There is much to be hopeful for, despite the inevitable setbacks. Martin Luther King Jr. said, "We must accept finite disappointment but never lose infinite hope."[9] That's exactly why I believe that repair is possible. Congressman John Lewis, who marched with Dr. King, knows the power of hope and calls us to move forward by faith. Lewis says that "faith is being so sure of what the spirit has whispered in your heart that your belief in its eventuality is unshakable. Nothing can make you doubt that what you have heard will become a reality. Even if you do not live to see it come to pass, you know without one doubt that it will be. That is faith."[10]

This type of faith cannot be maintained in isolation. To be able to keep the faith, we need each other. It's in the safety and solidarity of a loving and supportive community that we are able to withstand the criticism, opposition, and potential threat that will come. What is happening in the world is beyond a social or political reality; it is evil. In its roots, there is a spiritual, demonic undercurrent, and as the followers of Jesus, the church must be in the work of reconciliation with others to see, name, and address this spiritual dimension. This is the responsibility of the church. We cannot abdicate our responsibility and role in this vital work. We are called to be the people of God who have the spiritual insight and authority to uproot and eradicate the underlying causes of the evil realities that are at work in our world today. As Christian reconcilers, we must choose to use our faith, according to the teaching of Scripture, to reimagine the world as it should be. That will require us to come out of our individualism and come together as a community to make and execute a plan based on a united vision for the future. In the context of community, we find the support, courage, and accountability to imagine and work toward a world different from the one we currently live in.

This Christian narrative of hope necessarily reframes what we think of as "success." Success is equated not with changing the things we seek to address but with a transformational hope fueled by an eschatological vision—the promised future that we can't yet see. It is our specific responsibility to communicate this vision and to remind people of it. This is our unique role as we continue in the work of reconciliation. We must live into our call as the people of God who are entrusted with the ministry of reconciliation. We are reconcilers! Author Austin Channing Brown captures our powerful and prophetic mission in a declaration that I have proudly displayed in my office.

We Are Reconcilers

We are a collective of change agents.
Bored by easy answers, we wrestle with hard questions.

We understand history can speak prophetically.
We push ourselves purposefully.
We read voraciously, listen intentionally.
We act in solidarity. Often called troublemakers,
we interrupt the status quo.
We work to uproot white supremacy.
We hold power accountable, believing
in the possibility of change.
Working to dismantle unjust systems,
we drag injustice into the light.
We make peace. We promote truth and
love above politeness and civility.
We make noise because our lives depend on it.
We believe in reconciliation; we
recognize justice comes first.
We know God is working in the world. We celebrate.
We laugh. We honor one another. We practice joy.
Making room for grief, we cultivate hope.
We believe in redemption and resurrection.
We are confident in Love's victory.[11]

With this in mind, I now call all reconcilers to rise up! God is doing something great in the earth, and it's our time to seize the day. I hope that, through the pages of this book, you have received the necessary tools and encouragement to respond, like Esther, to God's leadership call in your life. I hope that our exploration of her life has helped create a new vision of socially relevant leadership that fuels your hope to pursue racial justice. I pray that your concept of reconciliation has been expanded to include more than just fellowship with those who may be different from you and that your expanded approach to race and racial justice centers on repair and not merely tolerance, inclusion, or appreciation. I hope you know that we must repair our interracial relationships through redressing the structures that mediate those relationships and harm our racial lives.

I hope you, as a reconciler, have strategies to make more than just a temporary, external difference. I sincerely want you to be able to create permanent and tangible changes that go far beyond a feel-good, relational moment, because that model of reconciliation is broken! Instead, I want us to repair the old reconciliation paradigm to make it more accurate and relevant for the era in which we currently find ourselves and for the time that is to come.

Most importantly, I hope you are inspired to become brave because great courage is needed in order to challenge the status quo and make the difference that is required of leaders in the twenty-first century. Esther embodied that courage, and it is a courage that comes from seeking God. So, as we end our journey, I am praying for you to be brave. I am praying that your courage is stirred, that your heart is open, and that your ears are receptive so that you can recognize the times in which we live and your very important part in bringing about the change that God seeks to accomplish in this world. Who knows? Maybe you were called to the kingdom of God for such a time as this!

One person can make a difference,
and everyone should try.

John F. Kennedy

ACKNOWLEDGMENTS

IT TOOK everything in me to write this book! To say that it was a labor of love would be an understatement. The birthing process was arduous and long, and I am truly grateful for the many people who helped this baby become a reality. First, I definitely want to thank my pastor-sister-friend, Gail Song Bantum, who read the first draft and called me to weave the narrative of my life throughout this book. Her insight and wisdom challenged me to dig deeper and be braver in speaking my truth. I am also sincerely thankful for my midwives on this project, Nancy Myers Rust and Sharisse Kimbro. They worked tirelessly as my writing assistants through every word of the manuscript until this baby was born. I am deeply indebted to them for their persistence and excellence in this work. I am also indebted to Ashley June Moore, Sarah Keough, Krystel Porter, Jonathan Roland, and Rebecca Weygandt. These reconcilers served as my readers and gave me invaluable feedback that greatly improved the relevance of this book. Thanks also to my friends, Roy Goble and Steve Stuckey, for their creative insights into the narrative of Esther. What a joy to glean from you! In addition, many thanks to my team at Brazos Press, especially Jeremy Wells, Kara Day, Paula Gibson, and Eric Salo, who believed in me and supported my vision throughout this project. Similarly, I am truly grateful for Matt Lewis (aka Hiro), whose creativity and direction fanned the flames of my imagination and helped to fulfill my vision for this work. My deepest thanks also goes to my intercessory prayer team—Barbara Brown, Nancy Sugikawa, Carol Roberts, Thomas Hurley, Rick Richardson, Rosanne Swain, and Joanne Jennings, who prayed over every aspect of this book and were an ongoing source of love and encouragement. No acknowledgment would be complete without thanking Carol Quinlan, my executive assistant, who supported me with excellence and made it possible for me to stay focused on writing this book. As always, my family has been in my corner throughout this entire process. A special shout-out goes to my son, Omari, who is my personal marketing and public relations consultant. I love you and am so grateful for your commitment to excellence in everything you do. In closing, I am so grateful this baby is finally here. Thanks be to God!

NOTES

Chapter 1: The Law of Timing

1. John Maxwell, *The 21 Irrefutable Laws of Leadership* (Nashville: Thomas Nelson, 1998).

Chapter 2: The Making of an Activist

1. "Religious Leaders Hold Peaceful Demonstration," Fox 32 News, November 30, 2015, https://www.fox32chicago.com/news/religious-lead ers-hold-peaceful-demonstration.

2. Ta-Nehisi Coates, *Between the World and Me* (New York: Spiegel & Grau, 2015), 133.

3. Deborah Jian Lee, "What Does Repentance Look Like for the White Church? A Conversation with Lisa Sharon Harper," Religion Dispatches, May 22, 2017, http://religiondispatches.org/what-does-repentance-look -like-for-the-white-church-a-conversation-with-lisa-sharon-harper.

4. Langston Hughes, "Mother to Son," in *The Collected Works of Langston Hughes* (Columbia: University of Missouri Press, 2002), https:// www.poetryfoundation.org/poems/47559/mother-to-son.

5. Brené Brown, *Rising Strong: How the Ability to Reset Transforms the Way We Live, Love, Parent, and Lead* (New York: Random House, 2015), 61.

Chapter 3: What Called You Forth?

1. Jennifer Harvey, *Dear White Christians* (Grand Rapids: Eerdmans, 2014).

2. Stuckey, "The Esther Paintings," StevenStuckey.com, http://www.stevenstuckey.com/making-art/art-blog.

3. Harriet Beecher Stowe, *Bible Heroines: Being Narrative Biographies of Prominent Hebrew Women in the Patriarchal, National, and Christian Eras, Giving Views of Women in Sacred History, as Revealed in the Light of the Present Day* (New York: Fords, Howard & Hulbert, 1878).

Chapter 4: When Politics Becomes Personal

1. Fidelis Mbah, "Nigeria's Chibok Schoolgirls: Five Years On, 112 Still Missing," *Al Jazeera*, April 14, 2019, https://www.aljazeera.com/news/2019/04/nigeria-chibok-school-girls-years-112-missing-1904131 92517739.html.

2. Greg Jao, "My daughters face lunchbox moments every week in a city as 'multicultural' as NYC," Facebook, May 4, 2016, https://www.facebook.com/greg.jao/posts/10156901438015188. Used with permission.

3. W. E. B. Du Bois, *The Souls of Black Folk* (New York: Gramercy, 1994), 3.

Chapter 5: Palace Living

1. Amy B. Wang, "'Post-truth' Named 2016 Word of the Year by Oxford Dictionaries," *Washington Post*, November 16, 2016, https://www.washingtonpost.com/news/the-fix/wp/2016/11/16/post-truth-named-20 16-word-of-the-year-by-oxford-dictionaries.

2. Mariam Khan and Luis Martinez, "More than 5,000 Muslims Serving in US Military, Pentagon Says," ABC News, December 8, 2015, http://abcnews.go.com/US/5000-muslims-serving-us-military-pentagon/story?id=35654904.

3. Toni Johnson, "Muslims in the United States," Council on Foreign Relations, September 19, 2011, https://www.cfr.org/backgrounder/muslims-united-states.

4. Charles Kurzman, "Muslim-American Terrorism in 2013," Triangle Center on Terrorism and Homeland Security, February 5, 2014, http://sites.duke.edu/tcths/files/2013/06/Kurzman_Muslim-American_Terror ism_in_20131.pdf.

5. Peter Holley, "Gun-Wielding Bandit Calls Indian Immigrant 'Terrorist' before Shooting Him in the Face," *Washington Post*, December 16, 2015, https://www.washingtonpost.com/news/morning-mix/wp/2015/12/15/gun-wielding-bandit-calls-indian-immigrant-terrorist-before-shootin g-him-in-the-face.

6. Corky Siemaszko, "Hate Attacks on Muslims in U.S. Spike after Recent Acts of Terrorism," NBC News, December 20, 2015, http://www

.nbcnews.com/news/us-news/hate-attacks-muslims-u-s-spike-after-re
cent-acts-terrorism-n482456; "Islamophobia: Understanding Anti-Muslim
Sentiment in the West," Gallup, accessed September 30, 2019, http://www
.gallup.com/poll/157082/islamophobia-understanding-anti-muslim-sen
timent-west.aspx.

7. Liam Stack, "American Muslims under Attack," *New York Times*,
February 15, 2016, http://www.nytimes.com/interactive/2015/12/22/us
/Crimes-Against-Muslim-Americans.html.

8. Nathan Rutstein, *Healing Racism in America: A Prescription for
the Disease* (Springfield, MA: Whitcomb, 1993), 99.

9. Robert J. Schreiter, *Reconciliation: Mission and Ministry in a
Changing Social Order* (Maryknoll, NY: Orbis Books, 1992), 34.

10. Schreiter, *Reconciliation*, 36.

11. Dashiell Bennett, "Americans Throw Away 40 Percent of Our
Food Every Day," *Atlantic*, August 22, 2012, https://www.theatlantic.com
/national/archive/2012/08/americans-throw-away-40-percent-our-food
-every-day/324433.

12. Eleanor Goldberg, "10 Things You Didn't Know about Slavery,
Human Trafficking (And What You Can Do about It)," *Huffington Post*,
January 15, 2014, updated December 6, 2017, http://www.huffingtonpost
.com/2014/01/15/human-trafficking-month_n_4590587.html.

13. Jennifer Harvey, *Dear White Christians* (Grand Rapids: Eerdmans,
2014), 59–60.

Chapter 6: The Prophetic Power of Lament

1. Jen Chung, "NYPD Strips Badge, Gun from Cop Involved in Fatal
Chokehold," *Gothamist*, July 20, 2014, https://gothamist.com/news/ny
pd-strips-badge-gun-from-cop-involved-in-fatal-chokehold.

2. Bethany Barnes, "DEAR BLACK COMMUNITY," Facebook, June
19, 2015, https://www.facebook.com/Barnes.Bethany/posts/4015055737
294. Used with permission.

3. Emmanuel Katongole and Chris Rice, *Reconciling All Things: A
Christian Vision for Justice, Peace and Healing* (Downers Grove, IL: IVP
Books, 2008), 77.

4. Katongole and Rice, *Reconciling All Things*, 77.

5. Katongole and Rice, *Reconciling All Things*, 78.

6. Ken Untener, "Prophets of a Future Not Our Own," United States
Conference of Catholic Bishops, accessed September 30, 2019, http://us
ccb.org/prayer-and-worship/prayers-and-devotions/prayers/prophets
-of-a-future-not-our-own.cfm.

Chapter 8: Healing the Disconnection

1. James Baldwin, *Conversations with James Baldwin* (Jackson: University Press of Mississippi, 1989), 156.

2. "Race and the Drug War," Drug Policy Alliance, accessed September 30, 2019, http://www.drugpolicy.org/race-and-drug-war; "The Drug War, Mass Incarceration and Race," Drug Policy Alliance, January 25, 2018, http://www.drugpolicy.org/resource/drug-war-mass-incarceratio n-and-race-englishspanish.

3. Dan Baum, "Legalize It All: How to Win the War on Drugs," *Harper's Magazine*, April 2016, https://harpers.org/archive/2016/04/legalize -it-all.

4. Hinton shared this story at the Faith Round Table at the Equal Justice Initiative, Montgomery, Alabama, 2015.

5. Bernice A. King (@BerniceKing), Twitter, May 14, 2017, https:// twitter.com/BerniceKing/status/863821217173843968?s=09.

6. Bryan Stevenson, "We Need to Talk about an Injustice," TED, March 2012, https://www.ted.com/talks/bryan_stevenson_we_need_to_talk _about_an_injustice/transcript.

7. See www.stolpersteine.eu/en/home.

8. Kay Campbell, "Bryan Stevenson: How to Build a Just Criminal-Justice System? Proximity, Narrative, Hope, Doing Uncomfortable Things," AL.com, November 4, 2014, updated March 5, 2019, https://www.al.com /living/2014/11/bryan_stevenson_huntsville.html.

Chapter 9: Breaking Our Silence

1. Jodi Picoult, *Small Great Things* (New York: Ballantine, 2016), 460–61.

2. The origins of this poem can be traced to Martin Niemöller (speech to the representatives of the Confessing Church, Frankfurt, Germany, January 6, 1946), https://en.wikiquote.org/wiki/Martin_Niem%C3% B6ller.

3. Diane Chapman Walsh, *Trustworthy Leadership: Can We Be the Leaders We Need Our Students to Become?* (Kalamazoo, MI: Fetzer Institute, 2006), 4, available at https://fetzer.org/sites/default/files/images /resources/attachment/2012-07-12/walshcovertext.pdf.

4. George Yancy, "I Am a Dangerous Professor," *New York Times*, November 30, 2016, https://www.nytimes.com/2016/11/30/opinion/i-am -a-dangerous-professor.html.

5. Frederick Buechner, *Secrets in the Dark* (New York: HarperCollins, 2006), 290.

Chapter 10: Intercessors for Justice

1. Walter Brueggemann, *The Creative Word: Canon as a Model for Biblical Education*, 2nd ed. (Minneapolis: Fortress, 2015), 52.
2. Martin Luther King Jr., *The Autobiography of Martin Luther King Jr.*, ed. Clayborne Carson (New York: IPM/Warner, 2001), https://swap .stanford.edu/20141218230026/http://mlk-kpp01.stanford.edu/kingweb /publications/autobiography/chp_8.htm.
3. Sarah Pulliam Bailey, "White Evangelicals Voted Overwhelmingly for Donald Trump, Exit Polls Show," *Washington Post*, November 9, 2016, https://www.washingtonpost.com/news/acts-of-faith/wp/2016/11/09 /exit-polls-show-white-evangelicals-voted-overwhelmingly-for-donald -trump.
4. Walter Brueggemann, *The Prophetic Imagination* (Minneapolis: Fortress, 2001), 3.
5. Austin Channing Brown, *I'm Still Here: Black Dignity in a World Made for Whiteness* (New York: Convergent, 2018), 181.

Chapter 11: Speaking Truth to Power

1. Quoted in Robert I. Fitzhenry, *The Harper Book of Quotations* (New York: HarperCollins, 1993), 356.
2. Ian Landau, "An Interview with Nobel Peace Prize Winner Leymah Gbowee," *Reader's Digest*, October 2011, https://www.rd.com/true -stories/inspiring/an-interview-with-nobel-peace-prize-winner-leymah -gbowee.
3. "The South Africa Kairos Document 1985," September 25, 1985, http://oikoumene.net/fix/file/dokumente/The%20South%20Africa%20 Kairos%20Document%201985.pdf.
4. W. E. B. Du Bois, *Prayers for Dark People*, ed. Herbert Aptheker (Amherst: University of Massachusetts Press, 1980), 21. Reprinted with permission of University of Massachusetts Press.

Chapter 12: The Reconciling Power of Women

1. Daniel Estrin, "Novelist Ayelet Waldman Is Sending Writers to the West Bank to Document What They See, 50 Years into Occupation," Public Radio International, May 1, 2016, http://www.pri.org/stories /2016-04-29/after-trying-ignore-israel-20-years-novelist-ayelet-waldman -sending-writers-there.
2. Ada María Isasi-Díaz, *Mujerista Theology: A Theology for the Twenty-First Century* (Maryknoll, NY: Orbis Books, 1996), 132.

3. Glennon Doyle Melton, *Love Warrior: A Memoir* (New York: Flatiron Books, 2016), 222–23.

4. Julia Gillard and Cate Blanchett, "Educate Women and Their Community Will Prosper. Deny Them Education and the World Will Suffer," *Guardian*, September 30, 2014, https://www.theguardian.com/comment isfree/2014/oct/01/educate-women-and-their-community-will-prosper -deny-them-education-and-the-world-will-suffer.

5. "Tawakkol Karman," Wikipedia, accessed January 19, 2020, https:// en.wikipedia.org/wiki/Tawakkol_Karman.

6. Langston Hughes, "I, Too," in *The Collected Works of Langston Hughes* (Columbia: University of Missouri Press, 2002), available at https://www.poetryfoundation.org/poems/47558/i-too.

7. Alexia Salvatierra and Peter Heltzel, *Faith-Rooted Organizing: Mobilizing the Church in Service to the World* (Downers Grove, IL: IVP Books, 2014), 74, 183.

8. Howard Thurman, *Jesus and the Disinherited* (Boston: Beacon, 1976), 31.

9. Thurman, *Jesus and the Disinherited*, 26.

10. Rabbi Yehiel E. Poupko, "Eating as a Celebration of Jewish Life," November 26, 2007, https://www.juf.org/news/thinking_torah.aspx?id =28094.

11. John M. Perkins, *Let Justice Roll Down* (Ventura, CA: Regal Books, 1976), 164–65.

12. Robert J. Schreiter, *Reconciliation: Mission and Ministry in a Changing Social Order* (Maryknoll, NY: Orbis Books, 1992), 60.

Conclusion

1. I used African Ancestry (http://www.africanancestry.com), the only Black-owned company that is considered a world leader in ancestry testing. It has the largest DNA database for people of African descent.

2. Henri Nouwen, *Bread for the Journey: A Daybook of Wisdom and Faith* (New York: HarperCollins, 2006), entry for June 14.

3. Willie James Jennings and Mark Labberton, "Can 'White' People Be Saved?" (lecture, Fuller Missiology Lectures, Fuller Theological Seminary, Pasadena, CA, November 2017), https://youtu.be/9wRvaG9j53g.

4. Monnica T. Williams, "Can Racism Cause PTSD? Implications for DSM-5," May 20, 2013, https://www.psychologytoday.com/blog/cultur ally-speaking/201305/can-racism-cause-ptsd-implications-dsm-5.

5. Sharon Pian Chan, "The Yellowface of 'The Mikado' in Your Face," *Seattle Times*, July 13, 2014, updated July 25, 2014, http://www.seattletimes .com/opinion/the-yellowface-of-ldquothe-mikadordquo-in-your-face.

6. Paul Taylor et al., "Wealth Gaps Rise to Record Highs between Whites, Blacks and Hispanics," Pew Research Center, July 26, 2011, http://citeseerx.ist.psu.edu/viewdoc/download?doi=10.1.1.397.5775&rep=rep1&type=pdf.

7. Alisa Valdes, "Is Your Child Gifted? Latino Kids Less Likely to Be Properly Diagnosed," Mamiverse, July 1, 2014, http://mamiverse.com/is-your-child-gifted-latino-kids-less-likely-to-be-properly-diagnosed-3526.

8. Amnesty International, "Maze of Injustice: The Failure to Protect Indigenous Women from Sexual Violence in the USA," 2007, https://www.amnestyusa.org/reports/maze-of-injustice.

9. Martin Luther King Jr., *In My Own Words*, ed. Coretta Scott King (London: Hodder & Stoughton, 2002).

10. John Lewis, *Across That Bridge: Life Lessons and a Vision for Change* (New York: Hachette, 2012), 20.

11. Austin Channing Brown, "We Are Reconcilers," AustinChanning.com, accessed November 19, 2019, https://static1.squarespace.com/static/50e26f21e4b0c2f4976dc211/t/55a5adbfe4b0f39d4454d1c2/1436921279193/Manifesto_turq.pdf. Used with permission.